THE PARKER MASTER GUIDE

TO

PERSONAL AND BUSINESS

SUCCESS

THE PARKER MASTER GUIDE

TO

PERSONAL AND BUSINESS

SUCCESS

Edited and compiled
by **Lawrence Talbott**

Parker Publishing Company, Inc.

West Nyack, N.Y.

© 1981 by

PARKER PUBLISHING COMPANY, INC.

West Nyack, N.Y.

Library of Congress Cataloging in Publication Data
Main entry under title:

Parker master guide to personal and business success.

Includes index.
1. Success—Addresses, essays, lectures.
2. Success—Case studies—Addresses, essays, lectures.
I. Talbott, Lawrence.
HF4386.P263   650.1   81-3929
ISBN 0-13-650291-1   AACR2

Printed in the United States of America

HOW TO MANAGE YOUR CAREER AND PERSONAL LIFE FOR GREATER GROWTH AND SECURITY, NO MATTER WHAT THE CONDITIONS

I'm sure that you'd never dream of going without insurance against accidents, illness and other calamities. Yet, you may be running a far greater risk against which you can't even buy an insurance policy—the problem of trying to succeed in a rapidly changing world with yesterday's (or even today's) skills. Fortunately, all the success insurance you will ever need is right here—on every page of this book.

When I undertook the editorship of *The Parker Master Guide to Personal and Business Success*, I read well over a million words in books that ranged in scope from basic self-improvement to the mysterious ways successful people train and use their minds. I wanted to see just what was available for motivated people like you. My goal was to uncover all the nuggets, the elements of success that anyone can use, not only to be up-to-date, but to remain out front in a world of change.

I found them. I found a solid core of practical and easy-to-use success secrets. But even more than this, I have been able to use all this information to create a program that anyone can use to insure that his or her skills for life and work will always be ahead of the challenge.

Whether you work for someone, own your own business, or are in the process of framing your life's plans at this very moment, this book will provide the fresh ideas, techniques and motivation you need to make it big. It's a one-stop source of carefully selected, practical plans and actions that have been tested over and over by those whose names are always mentioned whenever wealthy, powerful people are discussed.

As I interviewed successful people and read the writings of others, it became very clear to me that the skills each possessed could be divided into three basic categories. Those who hit the high notes in life and work had all developed their *mental, people* and *practical* skills to the point where they felt comfortable in any situation. Note that I said *felt* comfortable. You and I know that it is impossible to know everything and anticipate every event that leads to success. But, like the lawyer who knows enough to go to the correct reference when information is needed, you, too, can have at your fingertips the one collection of information that has helped make fortunes for so many others.

I have called this an *accelerated* success program. I can explain this by telling you about a person who should have succeeded many years before he actually did. Charlie Hansen was not a genius, but he did have a head on his shoulders. He had his share of ups and downs. But Charlie never made it really big until he discovered that the people he tried to influence with his ideas really didn't have a terribly high opinion of him.

Through no fault of his own, Charlie was low key. He seldom raised his voice, even when he should have. And he simply wasn't able to muster the enthusiasm needed to convince others that his ideas could succeed. They reasoned that if Charlie hadn't made it big, there was little likelihood that his ideas would.

When Charlie read one section from this book, he discovered just what he was doing wrong and what he had to do to turn the situation into a winning game. And he did all this in a matter of minutes. That is, he became aware of the problem in the few minutes he had the material, and in a few days he put the information into action and made enough in his first deal to carry him for three years. During those three years Charlie didn't sit back; he sharpened his other skills and has gone on to make several fortunes.

You'll meet many people like Charlie as you read this book. When you read their stories you will be able to accelerate your rise to success. After all, you probably have laid most of the ground work and don't even realize it. You will see how your previous efforts, regardless of their success or failure can be turned into roaring successes.

Now, let me tell you specifically how you are going to benefit from this book right away.

- You will learn how to identify those people who can help you succeed—and you will learn how to assure yourself of their help.

- You will learn how to cut through communications barriers, not only to understand others, but to make sure that your ideas become a part of their thinking.

- You will learn how to unleash a power that is within everyone—Kinesics—and you will be able to use it to achieve all the power, wealth and influence over people you have ever wanted.

- You will learn how to have instant memory power—a force that will permit you to remember complicated facts and figures with ease.

- You will learn how to break down the pyschological barriers that prevent people from doing what you want them to do.

- You will learn the secrets of Mental Dynamics, a force so powerful that it will increase your thinking, observation, listening, and reading skills overnight.

- It's just as easy to think big as to think small, and the rewards are a hundred times more important. You will learn how to reorient your attitudes and goals to encompass the big goals, the goals that pay off like nothing else.

- You will be shown exactly how to get maximum effort and productivity from everyone who can influence your climb to the top.

- You will be given the mental leverage you need to move yourself into the minds of the millionaires.

- You will be given the natural laws of effective communications—techniques that work quickly and effectively to help you influence every person with whom you come into contact.

- You will be given the keys you need to get the action you want from people—when you want it.

- You will see how easy it is to motivate people with the words you write.

- You will see how others have done so much in such a short period of time, and you will learn how to manage your time in order to do the same thing.

Sounds like a lot, doesn't it? Well, it is, but all of this and more only takes up 231 pages. Now I'm sure you can see why this is called

The Master Guide to Personal and Business Success. It's the heart of every success technique that has ever been used and found to work.

I want you to know that the years that have gone into the words you are about to read could add up not only to a college degree, but to several advanced degrees as well. And the information is complete, documented with case histories, and explained in terms that are not only meaningful, but positively motivational. Those who have read advance copies of this program claimed that it was like reading an adventure story, except that the characters were real people who were making big money, achieving what they set out to do and feeling very well-satisfied with themselves.

I promise you that you will feel the same. And I further promise that this book will help you in your career, your business and in all your relations with others to the point where you will be what you always wanted to be.

Lawrence Talbott

ACKNOWLEDGMENTS

Parker Publishing Company gratefully acknowledges permission to include in the PARKER MASTER GUIDE TO PERSONAL AND BUSINESS SUCCESS chapters and adaptations from the following books:

1. HOW TO LOCATE AND CULTIVATE THE PEOPLE WHO HAVE THE POWER TO HELP YOU SUCCEED

   James K. Van Fleet, *Power With People* (West Nyack, N.Y.: Parker Publishing Company, Inc., 1970).

2. HOW TO COMMAND ATTENTION FROM ANYONE, ANYTIME

   Edward J. Hegarty, *Making What You Say Pay Off* (West Nyack, N.Y.: Parker Publishing Company, Inc., 1968).

3. HOW TO GET INSTANT AND WILLING COOPERATION FROM ANYONE

   Merlyn Cundiff, *Kinesics: The Power of Silent Command* (West Nyack, N.Y.: Parker Publishing Company, Inc., 1972).

4. HOW TO USE THE NINE MEMORY POWER TACTICS TO MULTIPLY YOUR ABILITY TO CONCENTRATE

   David V. Lewis, *The Miracle of Instant Memory Power* (West Nyack, N.Y.: Parker Publishing Company, Inc., 1973).

5. HOW TO MULTIPLY YOUR IMPACT ON PEOPLE AND BE MASTER OF EVERY SITUATION

   Les Donaldson, *How to Use Psychological Leverage to Double the Power of What You Say* (West Nyack, N.Y.: Parker Publishing Company, Inc., 1978).

6. HOW TO MOVE AHEAD EFFORTLESSLY BY THINKING LIKE A LEADER

   David J. Schwartz, *The Magic of Thinking Big* (Englewood Cliffs, N.J.: Prentice-Hall, Inc., 1959).

7. HOW TO MULTIPLY YOUR PERSONAL GROWTH POWER BY THINKING BIG

Schwartz, *The Magic of Thinking Big.*

8. HOW TO USE THE MASTER "POWER PLAY" IN EVERY PERSONAL SITUATION

James K. Van Fleet, *Van Fleet's Master Guide for Managers* (West Nyack, N.Y.: Parker Publishing Company, Inc., 1978).

9. HOW TO CHART AND CASH IN ON YOUR PERSONAL SUCCESS CYCLE

Howard E. Hill, *How to Think like a Millionaire and Get Rich* (West Nyack, N.Y.: Parker Publishing Company, Inc., 1968).

10. HOW TO PERSUADE PEOPLE TO DO JUST WHAT YOU WANT THEM TO DO

James A. Morris, Jr., *The Art of Conversation: The Magic Key to Personal and Social Popularity* (Englewood Cliffs, N.J.: Prentice-Hall, Inc., 1976).

11. HOW TO COME OUT ON TOP IN EVERY PEOPLE-HANDLING SITUATION YOU WILL EVER FACE

A. G. Strickland, *How to Get Action: Key to Successful Management* (Englewood Cliffs, N.J.: Prentice-Hall, Inc., 1975).

12. HOW TO GET THE RESULTS YOU WANT WITH EVERY LETTER YOU WRITE

William M. Parr, *Executive's Guide to Effective Letters and Reports* (West Nyack, N.Y.: Parker Publishing Company, Inc., 1976).

13. HOW TO WIN WITH WORDS THAT EVERYBODY KNOWS, USES AND UNDERSTANDS

Duane Newcomb, *Word Power Makes the Difference: Making What You Write Pay Off* (Englewood Cliffs, N.J.: Prentice-Hall, Inc., 1975).

14. HOW TO CONTROL AND PERSONALLY BENEFIT FROM EVERY MOMENT OF YOUR TIME

Sydney F. Love, *Mastery and Management of Time* (Englewood Cliffs, N.J.: Prentice-Hall, Inc., 1978).

CONTENTS

11

How to Locate
and Cultivate Those
Who Have the Power
to Help You Succeed*

1

All of us have at least two major goals in life: *Success* and *Happiness*. And you've taken the first big step toward gaining both of them when you realize that your getting success and happiness depends on other people.

Yes, it's a proven fact. You simply cannot succeed in life without the help of other people. If you want to get ahead in this old world, you must get other people on your side.

You must get them to push for you, stand up for you, cheer for you, vote for you—yes, even fight for you, to stick with you all the way. The best way for you to get ahead is to use your personal power to influence and control—to master and dominate—*certain key people, specific individuals who can help you achieve success in life.* You must find out—*which people can help you the most.*

"It marks an important point in your progress when you realize that other people can help you do a better job than you can do alone," says George T. Vanderhoff, president of Holland Industries, Inc., of Holland, Michigan.

"But you'll really make a giant stride forward in your efforts to succeed when you know who these key individuals are who can really help you become successful.

---

*James K. Van Fleet, *Power With People* (West Nyack, N.Y.: Parker Publishing Company, Inc., 1970).

"Actually, this ought to be your very first goal: *to find out which people can help you most*. Do that, and you'll benefit tremendously by saving time and energy when you *concentrate your efforts only on those people who can help you achieve your goals*. To devote your attention to anyone else is a complete waste of time!"

BENEFITS YOU'LL GAIN

When you pinpoint those people who can help you become successful, you'll realize many benefits—that's precisely what I want to tell you about next: the advantages George says you'll gain when you concentrate only on those key individuals who can help you attain your goals and become successful. Here's what they are:

You'll Control People

You'll be able to control many people through just a few. You don't need to control the whole human race to be successful. But you can control dozens of people—yes, even hundreds—through just a few key people.

Genghis Khan controlled his vast far-flung empire through certain key people—his loyal tribal chieftains. His was a military empire won by armed conquest. But the same principle of control applies to the economic empire of General Motors. The president of GM is head of an organization that has more than three quarters of a million employees. He could not possibly control this modern sprawling economic giant without the help of key officers and able administrators.

You'll Save Time

You'll save time when you concentrate your efforts on the right person. Time is important to all of us. It's a successful salesman's most valuable asset. He'll never waste it by giving his sales pitch to someone who can't make the buying decision. There's a saying among successful salesmen: *Sell the secretary on seeing her boss; sell him on buying your product.*

Ask any business executive what his greatest problem is, and he'll tell you, "Not enough time in a day to get everything done." That's why he carries a briefcase home every night. If you're like the rest of us—and it doesn't matter whether you're a business executive, a college student, a teacher, or a housewife—you no doubt have the same problem. There just isn't enough time to get everything done. But you can solve most of this problem by concentrating on the person who can help you do the job. Don't waste your time on the person who can't help you!

You'll Save Energy

You'll save energy and effort when you pinpoint the pivot man. This is particularly useful to those who work with large groups of people: teachers and preachers; supervisors and foremen; military officers and industrial leaders. But its value isn't limited to those individuals alone. If you work with as few as two other people—and it doesn't matter whether it's on your job or with the finance committee in your church—these techniques can be useful to you, too.

Pivot people are always action people. Their personalities demand action and lots of it. They stagnate in humdrum, routine, monotonous jobs. Learn who the pivot people are in your group; you'll get far better results when you do. Pivot people are especially important to you when you need action and you need it right now. They can help you get that action when and where you most need it. Working under pressure comes naturally to them.

You'll Be Halfway to Success

Find the key person to help you gain your objectives, and you're well over halfway on the road to success. Russell Conwell's lecture, *Acres of Diamonds*,* is probably the most famous speech in the history of the American lecture platform. Although its message will always be inspiring and pertinent, part of its fame came from Dr. Conwell's unique methods.

Dr. Conwell always arrived in a town far ahead of his scheduled speaking time. He would visit the postmaster, the school principal, the mayor, local ministers, prominent businessmen, and other key figures

---

*Russell Conwell, *Acres of Diamonds* (Westwood, N.J., Fleming H. Revell Co., 1960).

in the town. He won these people to his side long before he stepped to the platform; they helped him win the rest of the people.

You can do the same, whether you're talking to parents at a PTA meeting; speaking to the Thursday night bowling league; attending a meeting of the town council; or addressing the board of directors in a closed conference room. Find the key people and get 'em on your side first; the rest will automatically follow.

You'll Become "King"

Find the power behind the throne and you can become king! Key people are often far removed from any official position of authority or responsibility. They will have an aura of influence far out of proportion to their position in the organization. They'll be the unofficial leaders, the pushers, the instigators, but they'll never be out in front in plain view. Their work all takes place behind the scenes. You must find them; you must know who they are, for you need them on your side to become successful.

TECHNIQUES YOU CAN USE
TO GAIN THE BENEFITS

Find the Boss in the House

Every day, a great many decisions, both business and social, are made that require a joint decision of husband and wife. PTA meetings often boil down to a triangle of father, mother, and teacher. Insurance salesmen and real estate salesmen, as well as car salesmen, face this same problem of getting a husband and wife to see eye to eye on their propositions.

I'm sure you've found yourself in a situation where the husband and wife must make a decision together. Even though both of them might have to say "Yes," or both of them might have to sign the same document, only one will be the key persom—the right target for you to aim at.

The question is—which person is it, and how do you find out? I want to show you how a couple of others run into this same problem, and how they solve it, so you'll know how to do it, too.

   A *salesman finds the real boss in the house.* Bob Gallivan, one of
the most outstanding life insurance salesmen to come down the pike in
a long, long time, and author of *How I Started Earning $50,000 a
Year in Sales at the Age of 26**, has this to say about the role of the
woman in making decisions about her husband's life insurance:

   "The wife is the key to how much insurance the husband will
ultimately buy," Bob says. "On my first visit, I always concentrate on
her to confirm that fact. I always question her first, using her given
name: 'Mary, what benefits do you expect to get from pensions and
social security?' Invariably, Mary has to ask her husband.

   "Not only that, I find that most wives have no idea where such
vital papers as birth certificates, marriage licenses, wills, insurance
policies, and other important documents are kept. Many don't know
how to detect tell-tale signs of car trouble; others have no idea of how
or where to get the most for their dollar—be it groceries or clothing.

   "I do all this to show a wife how helpless she'd be without her
husband if something should suddenly happen to him. I insist that she
do all the figuring when we get down to the point of how much
insurance her husband should have. *This is vital!* For the first time in
years, perhaps, Mary has become a big part of the financial core of the
family.

   "When I'm all through, I can guarantee you one thing. The
husband may pay the premiums, but the wife bought his policy!"

   I'm sure you noticed one thing here in Bob's method of determining the boss in the house. *He himself, makes the wife the key person! He
makes her the boss, at least, for this one small moment of time.* And she
takes immediate advantage of the opportunity he's given her; she may
never get the chance again!

   Not every life insurance salesman can use this approach and
make it work, but there's no better one if you can pull it off. It requires
skill, experience, and a great deal of tact to use it successfully. I've seen
furniture salesmen earn forty thousand a year and more by making a
backward little house-mouse into a VIP for just a few minutes of time.

   Try this new tactic yourself the next time you have to deal with a
husband and wife where a joint decision is required. You'll find it will

---

   *Bob Gallivan, *How I Started Earning $50,000 a Year in Sales at the Age of 26*
(Englewood Cliffs, N.J., Prentice-Hall, Inc., 1963).

work wonders for you. Teachers and preachers find it especially useful, too. However, it's not the best approach for selling real estate, as you'll find out when you listen to the following story.

A *real estate salesman and the husband-wife combination.* Dale Wells, sales manager for the Fred Myers Company, Des Moines, Iowa, says this about how to handle the married couple in the real estate business:

"A real estate salesman has one of the oddest of all jobs in the selling game. First of all, he has to sell two people on the idea of selling their house. Then he has to sell two more people on the idea of buying it. Altogether, he has to satisfy a minimum of four people, and if the buyers have children, the number of people to be satisfied becomes even greater.

"When I'm trying to get a listing, that is, when I want a couple to let me sell their house for them, I watch the reactions of both of them very carefully. I use a lot of questions to see who will speak up first and to find out which one will turn to the other for an answer.

"If I ask 'How much did you plan on getting for your house?' and John turns to Martha and says, 'What do you think, dear?', I'm pretty sure she's the key to my getting that listing. But I'll follow that one up with more questions. I might ask 'How soon would you be able to move after your house is sold?' Again, if the wife answers, I'm almost dead certain she wears the pants in that house. Here's one that will usually clinch it for me:

" 'Does this window air conditioner stay with the house?' I ask.

" 'Absolutely not!' she snaps. '*I'm* taking it with *us!*'

"Well, no doubt about it now. She's the key to my getting the listing in this case. Papa may bring home the bread, but Mama decides how and when it's going to be eaten! If she signs on the dotted line—so will he.

"I use much the same questioning technique to find the spokesman for the buyers. 'How many bedrooms do you need? Is the living room adequate for you? Isn't this a beautiful family room?' It doesn't take too long to find out who's running that household, either.

"On the average, though, I've found that on the buyer's side, if you can satisfy the husband with the price and the wife with the house, you'll usually close your sale."

Bridegrooms need to know who's boss, too! Now it could well be that asking a girl's parents for their daughter's hand is completely out-of-date, but getting them to approve of you first will still remove a lot of stones from your marital path.

When I married my "first wife," it was still the custom to introduce the prospective in-laws to each other on some sunny Sunday afternoon so they could size each other up and find out about their religion, their politics, their drinking habits, and their economic and social status.

On just such an occasion when my future in-laws were meeting my parents for the first time, my mother took me aside in her kitchen and said, "You're trying to sell the wrong person, son. Her mother's already sold on you. You don't have to soft-soap her any longer. Now go after her father; he's the key figure. He's the one you need to convince, for he makes the decisions in that house—not her. She just came along for the ride!"

And with that instinctive woman's intuition, my mother was right. He was the key figure and getting his approval was tough. We've been married more than 25 years now, and I'm still working on it. Of course, it might have helped if we'd waited a little longer for his decision back in the beginning and not eloped! (Incidentally, just in case you're wondering, I'm still married to my "first wife." You see, I always introduce her that way. Even after more than 25 years of marriage, it helps keep her on her toes!)

How to Find the Key Man in Groups

Pinpointing the people who can help you can be a little tougher proposition than finding the key figure in a couple. And the more people there are in the group, the harder you'll have to look to find the key individual. But have patience; it can be done.

Take the average business, for example. Every company always has a few people who wield an influence that has no relapionship whatever to their vested authority or their actual position. It's up to you to find out who they are. They can make you or break you whether you like to admit that or not. Here are some of the clues you can use to spot these key people you need on your side.

The pivot man is independent. You can usually spot a pivot man by his need for independent action. Often, this pivot personality or key individual will be a man or woman who has refused a position of leadership or supervision—even though he apparently has all the necessary qualifications—because he doesn't want to be pinned down by official responsibility.

A *pivot man solves problems.* A pivot man often has a solution for your problem. A great many times the hardest part of solving any problem is simply getting on it. A pivot man can help you get that action when you need it most. He'll often have several suggestions for solving your problems. His ideas are not always the best, but they will help get something moving in a bogged-down situation.

The key man is a creative thinker. A pivot man is usually a creative thinker—a non-conformist. A really creative personality will resist strongly any efforts to restrict and channel his thinking. If his creative urge is strong enough, it will show up in his efforts to get transferred to new jobs, or, at least, to acquire additional knowledge of other departments and other people's work. This may well be your first clue to the presence of a pivot man—a key personality who can help you achieve your goals.

Others rely on him for help. Other members of the group turn to him for advice and help. A supervisor issues an order, turns his back, and walks away. Immediately, the workers gather around one individual. He speaks; they listen. Then they go back to work and carry out the supervisor's order. *But not until they get the unofficial go-ahead from the informal leader of the group!*

When You Know Him, Use the Key Man to Your Advantage

Once you've found the key man in your group, you can use him as your unofficial transmitter. You can feel out your group by taking him aside and getting his opinion first. This doesn't make him the boss; it simply gets him on your side. Remember the basic rule: *Find out who the key people are and get 'em on your side first; the rest will automatically follow.*

Above all, don't lock horns with the key man if you're the group's official leader. There's nothing wrong with his influence in the group just as long as he doesn't misuse his power and try to usurp yours. You'll get much further with your group if you work with him and *learn how to use his power with the group by turning it to your own advantage; use it for your own benefit.*

Finding the Key Figure Is Important to Industry

"If you're a foreman of a department as I am, or a supervisor, you must know the key people you can depend on," says Bill Kessler, with General Electric's Toledo, Ohio plant. "Then you've got to put them into your key spots—your critical production jobs—so they can watch your danger areas for you.

"I have a man like that on my production line named Hugh Atwood. He can provide the leverage for my department when I need it most. Hugh can make or break the quality image of GE with his soldering iron for he's in a key spot and the movement of the product down the line depends entirely upon him.

"Fortunately for all of us, Hugh has a lot of pride in doing a job well. And he spreads his desire for excellence throughout my entire department. His ability to inspire others along the line to do a better job is worth more to the company than a dozen quality control men checking the end product.

"Yet he's refused promotion time after time. 'Don't want to get all bound up with rules and regulations and red tape the way you do, Bill,' he says. 'You and your management boys can worry about that; I just want to work on turning out a good product for you, Bill.' "

Strange for a man to refuse a promotion? Not at all. Remember, *it's one of the clues to finding that pivot man.* I've known career officers in the service, graduates of West Point, to resign from the army simply because of the command line of red tape that strangles creative thought. The result? The army's losing valuable officers—key people—to civilian business and industry simply because they haven't learned how to identify them and how to handle them. *They haven't learned how to pinpoint the people who can help them until it's too late!*

"I'd make a heck of a poor fisherman," Colonel Wayne Zellers told me. "My job is to sell young officers on staying in the army and making it a career. Trouble is, I always let the best ones get away!"

Finding the pivot man is important in business, too. "We want to develop our key management people to the maximum." says Lee

Summers, vice president in charge of executive development and training with Phillips Petroleum Company in Kansas City, Missouri. "We shift them from one position to another at definite fixed intervals so they can gain the greatest experience possible and develop a broad and knowledgeable background.

"We do try to locate these key personalities as soon as we can for two reasons: First, the sooner we start developing a man, the better for both of us. Second, we don't want to waste time and money on the wrong individual."

The supervisor who's caught in the middle. No doubt about it; most people in business or industry today are in positions that require the utmost tact and diplomacy in working with other people. Even the last man in the management line has to be an expert in human relations.

Take Marvin Powers, for instance. He's a front-line supervisor for the Gold Seal Trailer Company, one of the leading manufacturers in the United States of travel trailers and other recreational vehicles. Marvin is the last link in the management chain. He's the immediate supervisor of the production employee. And he's usually caught right in the middle. If ever anyone needs to know who the key people are who can help him, it's Marvin! Listen to his story as he told it to me:

"I don't know which way to jump," Marvin says. "I have to please everybody: the production superintendent, industrial engineering, quality control, the budgeting and cost accounting people, other department foremen, the men in my own section. But I just can't do it; I can't please them all!

"If I speed up my department's output so that all other production employees in the plant can work at top speed, the incentive goes too high in my own section and the cost accounting people get on my back. Or if my machinery runs too fast, the quality goes down, and the quality control people buck stuff back to me because it isn't done right. When that happens, my own men get their paychecks docked for they get paid only for quality production—not for scrap. Then they blame me for pushing them too hard!

"If I don't keep up with other departments' demands, then the production superintendent climbs my frame when they complain to him. Of course I know he has to keep the plant manager and the sales manager happy, too, as well as the big boys up in Elkhart, Indiana. But all that sure puts me right in the middle. It's just a big wicked cycle!"

I agree with Marvin—but only up to a point. His job does take a lot of know-how to keep everybody happy. But he can simplify his problem by keeping a couple of points in mind:

1. *Whom do I have to please to keep my job?*
2. *Whom do I have to please to get promoted?*

Now I'm not recommending that Marvin (or you either, if you're caught in similar circumstances) not try to please others, or that you make enemies by purposely stepping on other people's toes. The important point you should remember is this: *Who are the key people to be pleased, in this matter, above all others?* When Marvin answers that question, he'll be well on his way to solving the major part of his problem. And so will you.

Even Preachers Look for the Key Figure in the Group

"I am always willing that my church should raise my salary," says Samuel Thorne, pastor of the Central Methodist Church in St. Louis, Missouri. "Over the years I've found that the church that pays the largest salary always raises it the most easily. Based on that premise, I suppose I shouldn't worry about it right now. Still, it's something I've never dared take for granted.

"So when the time comes for the church to consider a salary increase for me, I concentrate my attention on the budget and finance committee to show them how easily we can afford my raise. I personally don't try to sell my whole congregation on the idea; the committee does that for me.

"But I've learned something else, too, through the years. Not all of the key figures are on that budget and finance committee. Keep your eye on that little old lady who says, 'I don't know why the girls always call on me for help and advice; really, I don't. I'm not on any of their committees. Of course, I'm always willing to do what I can to help out. In fact, whenever we're having a church supper, they always call me to ask what they can do!'

"I watch our for her, my friend. She's the one I'll need on my side to get that raise in salary. She's the power behind the throne!"

Colonel Zellers is right–the army does let the best ones get away! David Hall entered the army as a second lieutenant in 1951 having graduated from West Point in the top third of his class. He left the army as a Major in 1963, giving up his rank and his retirement benefits to go to work for an electronics firm in Los Angeles.

I know David personally; he is a good friend of mine. In my opinion, the army let one of its best future generals get away when he left. David has a brilliant mind and the ability to lead people. And he's ambitious. After his day's work with the electronics firm, he goes to school at night. He now has his master's degree, and is looking forward to forming his own company soon.

"I left the army for a lot of reasons, but one of the main ones was that I was never quite sure who I worked for or who had the final say-so on the subject. I simply got tired of trying to obey conflicting orders," David says.

"Theoretically, the chain of command is well established in the army. Yet I've served in outfits where I was never quite sure who I worked for or who was going to make out my efficiency report. The only time they were ever really sure of the chain of command was when someone had goofed and they wanted to pin the 'guilty' part and get the monkey off their own backs! It was sort of a pin-the-tail-on-the-donkey game.

"I always felt that if you want to be successful you must give your loyalty and your devotion to the man who makes out your fitness report. I still feel that way; that's why I left the army. I got tired of looking for that man.

"*You must know who the key people are in your life.* How else can you hope to succeed? And I don't mean politicking or applepolishing or some other term they use in the army I'd better not use here, perhaps. I do mean you should do your level best to please your boss. You should do a decent job for him. You ought to do everything in your power to make him look good. *He's the key man in your career.* Out here I know who that man is; in there I was never quite sure!"

Teachers, Too!

There's a young high school English teacher named Arch Spain I talk with a lot. In fact, I use him as a sounding board quite often, for he spends a lot of time at our house (not to see me, by the way, but to see my daughter, Teresa). I asked him how important it is for a teacher to locate the key students in his class. Here's what he says about it:

"Students today aren't interested in dead theory or moth-ball morality," he says. "They want to know how a certain subject will help them earn a living and how it will help them get along with people. I always try to impress them with the idea that they are the future of their little town. I tell them that without a doubt this very class has within it a mayor, members of the town council, important businessmen and women.

"And since they'll be spending most of their lives together trying to understand each other, they ought to learn how to communicate with each other right now. 'That's what English is for,' I tell them. 'To learn how to communicate; not just to learn how to conjugate verbs!' And to get them to communicate, I ask them for their own ideas and opinions about politics, government, racial problems, morality, church and religion, liquor, dope, and any number of current topics.

"This always brings out fresh ideas and immediate suggestions for improvement from at least two or three key people and soon the rest of the class dives in. From then on I gear everything to the thinking of those few key students, and I have the entire class in the palm of my hand in no time at all. Those few key people do what I want them to do. They step right out in front and the rest follow their lead without question."

Associate with the Right People

Not only does it make good sense to pinpoint the key people who can help you become successful, it's also wise to associate with them since they can help you get ahead. By the same token, it doesn't make much sense to cultivate the friendship of those who can do nothing for you. Why try to grow a crop of weeds?

Carl T., a good friend of mine, a recovered alcoholic and a member of Alcoholics Anonymous, brings this point out quite well, I think: "If I'd learned earlier in life to associate with the right people rather than a bunch of drunks, I'd never have ended up as an alcoholic," Carl says. "Now I've learned to cultivate the friendship of those people in Alcoholics Anonymous who can help me stay sober.

"After all, I didn't join AA to learn how to dance; I got on the program so I could learn how to get sober and stay sober. I never learned that from any of my drinking buddies!"

POINTS TO REMEMBER

The best way you can get ahead is to use your personal power to influence and control—to master and dominate *certain key people—specific individuals who can help you achieve success in life.* Do that and you'll gain these benefits:

1. You'll be able to control many people through just a few.
2. You'll save time by concentrating your efforts on the right person.
3. You'll save energy and effort by pinpointing the pivot man.
4. When you find the key person to help you gain your objectives, you're over halfway on the road to success.
5. Find the power behind the throne and you'll become king!

How to Gain These Benefits

1. Find the boss in the house.
2. Sell the boss—not his secretary.
3. Find the key man in groups.
4. Know for sure whom you have to please ABOVE ALL OTHERS.
5. Avoid the people who can't help you succeed.

How to Command Attention from Anyone, Anytime*

2

It's not easy to command attention, but you can succeed when you know how to get people to listen to you. You can make the job easier if you analyze the steps you and the listener go through in a speaker-listener situation.

STEPS IN THE LISTENER-SPEAKER SITUATION

1. Understand Your Listener.
2. Get His Favorable Attention.
3. Help Him Hear What You Say.
4. Make It Easier for Him to Understand.
5. Arouse His Interest.
6. Hold His Interest.
7. Show That You Like Him.
8. Let Him Like You.
9. Listen to Him.

---

*Edward J. Hegarty, *Making What You Say Pay Off* (West Nyack, N.Y.: Parker Publishing Company, Inc., 1968).

1. UNDERSTAND YOUR LISTENER

You know most of your listeners. They are your employees, your bosses, and your associates. You know too that every one of them is different. Each has ideas, thoughts, opinions, or foibles that can help shape your talk to him. Since you are the boss, you may think that your employees have to listen to you. "They had better or else," you say. But they listen better when you slant your speech so they can see what the proposal means to them. Don't spout off about your pet peeve—taxes. They don't want to listen to that subject. You may argue, "He should be interested." But few listeners will be interested because they should be.

Talk about his job, his work, his performance, his ambitions, and you have an interested listener.

Think of His Interests

On a piece of note paper copy the chart below. Now think of the other supervisors at your level in your company and check on your chart their interests in these recreations.

Recreation	Charlie	Jack	Timothy
golf			
bowling			
boating			
fishing			
baseball			
football			

The men are different, but your check shows they have interests in common. It is the same with groups. Each group has enough in common so that your appeal need not be too far off its interests. Your wife says she doesn't like your friend, Gus. You say, "Why not? He's a good guy." She answers, "All he can talk about is golf." Golf talk doesn't appeal to her interests. If he learned about her garden club and her girl scout troop and talked a bit about them she would no doubt listen to him and like him better.

Make a joke about one of the plans of management and it gets a big laugh from the fellows in the department. Make that same crack to your boss and it may get you a lecture on loyalty. He's been brain-washed more than the gang around you. He may say, "I like you, Gary, but cracks like that may make management wonder about you." Know your listener, use what you know about him, and what you say will have a better chance to PAY OFF.

2. GET HIS FAVORABLE ATTENTION

It does little good to speak if you don't get attention. You can yell, "Hey, You." The other person gets it, but this type of greeting does little else but attract attention and it won't be too favorable. Say, "Hear the one about the bartender and the turtle?" and you have attention. The writer is advised, "Get the reader's attention before he has time to turn the page." This is an idea to use in all PAYOFF conversation. Assume you want to tell the boss something. He wants to tell you something. You don't have much chance to explain your idea before he tells you what he wants to say. Perhaps he would have listened if you had started with, "Here's how we can cut costs." Use this idea with your boss, the help, anybody. Plan your first words.

Get Attention with This Type of Question

How often do you approach others with questions such as

1. Want to make some easy money?
2. Want to increase your profits?
3. Want to meet a nice-looking girl?
4. Want to cut costs?

You may not use these exact questions, but use the type of question that promises a benefit and you'll get attention.

3. HELP HIM HEAR WHAT YOU SAY

Much of the trouble in understanding speakers is in the listener not hearing what the speaker says. My first example of this is the way a man's name is pronounced when he is introduced. Usually the introducer comes up with, "I'd like you to meet my friend, Mr. Ump Ump." You know that is not his name, but that's what you heard. If your listener wants to hear and he doesn't hear, it's your fault.

Ask Yourself These Questions

1. Am I speaking loudly enough? If you have a weak voice, you may need to turn up the volume.
2. Do I speak too fast? Slow down and you can be sure he has a better chance of understanding.
3. Do I enunciate clearly? One word may become another if you don't.

If you have any of these faults, you are asking the listener to put out more effort than is needed to hear what you say. Advice given in later chapters will show you how to correct these faults.

4. MAKE IT EASIER FOR HIM TO UNDERSTAND

If he doesn't understand, he shrugs, "Well, it's your dime." But he feels you are at fault. He's not too dumb to understand. You are too dumb to make yourself clear. And that comes close to the truth.

How Do You Perform in the Following Areas?

1. Do you speak directly, using as few words as possible to express your idea?
2. Do you say specifically what you mean?
3. Do you take the time to repeat when you should?
4. Are you using words familiar to him, words he might use?

5. Are you using words that he might think have a different meaning from the one you want them to convey?

6. Is your subject too complicated for him?

These questions indicate many of the mechanical problems we face in speaking with others. If you are guilty of any of the faults mentioned, you are complicating the listener's life and yours.

5. AROUSE HIS INTEREST

After you have the listener's attention, your next job is to kindle his interest. You can't talk to Angus for long about a subject in which he has no interest. It pays to see his problems through *his* eyes. You want some information from him. To get it for you, he has to go through his files and dig out folders on each item. You are thinking about the information; he is thinking about the extra work involved in digging through those files. Try to anticipate any such complications. Your request might be more acceptable if you offer to help dig out the folders.

Check Your Skill at Arousing Interest

Let's say you want the shipping department to get out a special shipment to St. Louis this afternoon. If the order was handled in rotation the shipment would go out tomorrow afternoon, or even the next day. But you want it to go out today. What could you say to get the shipping boys interested in getting it out this afternoon? Think of three remarks.

Pause and think of three appeals before you read on. Here are three that men in my speech clinic have given:

1. "The speed will show the big shots what a fine shipping department we have."

2. "It will make a good impression on our general manager."

3. "The customer in St. Louis will think you boys are wizards."

This is the kind of talk that helps you get what you want. Think a bit before you ask any department to turn everything upside down to do what you want. Figure out some benefits they will receive and mention those benefits.

One man in my clinic said, "I offer to buy them a beer at quitting time." That's good too, but if you can show a more important benefit tell them about it. You know your listener is asking, "What do I get out of it?" Tell him and he will be more inclined to go along with what you want.

Use These Appeals You Hear Every Day on TV

1. It's easier.
2. Less work, saves time.
3. Does the job better.
4. Saves money.

Around the office use

5. Approval of the boss.
6. Good of the company.
7. Reputation of his department.
8. Pride in his work.

Not long ago there was a story in the newspapers about the Internal Revenue suing a TV luminary for $168,000 for back taxes. The next evening I heard a loudmouth in a bar arguing that it was OK for the big shot to cheat the Government on his income taxes if he could get away with it. Another fellow listened, then asked, "Oh, you're willing to pay the big shot's taxes for him?" That changed the picture, didn't it?

Let's apply this thinking to a simple problem. You want Chuck to go fishing with you next weekend. You know that when you suggest the trip he will immediately think of all the complications that going away for a weekend will entail. Thus you have to do some selling.

Which of These Sentences Will Appeal to Chuck?

1. You need the vacation.
2. The wife and kids need a vacation from you.
3. You haven't tried that new lure you got for Christmas.
4. The fish are biting.

5. You know how much fun we have at camp.

6. I got two bottles of Old Grandad.

7. I'll drive my car.

8. Remember that waitress up there.

Perhaps all of them will appeal, perhaps none, but it is certain that you will have less argument with Chuck if you include some benefits of this sort.

Do you usually use such appeals in your approach to others? Think back to a transaction you handled today with another department. OK, what appeals of this kind could you have used?

Pause and think out this problem before you read on. Don't tell me, "They know how they benefit." Perhaps they do, but again I say, "Don't assume. Tell them."

6. HOLD HIS INTEREST

In addition to appeal there are two considerations that affect the PAYOFF value of what you say to every listener.

(a) You speak more slowly than he listens.

(b) He has a certain span of attention.

(a) He Listens Faster than You Talk. We speak at a rate of 120 to 180 words per minute. We listen at 800 words per minute. Thus the listener is ahead of the speaker, miles ahead. If he doesn't sense the importance of what you say, his mind can go down to the bar on the corner for an imaginary small beer while you speak on. Words can lose attention. We speak words of doubtful meaning, ones like, "specious," or "precocity." His mind wanders searching for the meaning of that word. He has heard the word, but what does it mean?

Excess words also can do this. Say, "You may not agree with this," and his mind starts figuring out reasons why. Use a term that is not specific like "review this report" and he starts wondering what you mean. Remember it is easier for his mind to wander than to stay with your subject unless you use all the skill you have.

(b) His Mind Strays if You Talk Too Long: This is what happens during the sermon on Sunday. We all have a span of attention that varies with our interest in the subject, our knowledge of it, and our

difficulty of understanding. The other day in a meeting I heard one listener in the audience call, "Hold it, I want to digest that." The plea indicated that the speaker was going too fast. This seldom happens in a meeting or in a conversation. The listener allows you to go on without comment.

The Common Attention Losers

1. Talking too fast.
2. Talking too long.
3. Repetition of the story you told him yesterday and perhaps the day before.
4. Wordiness.
5. Talking a language he doesn't understand.
6. Failing to tell him why the subject is important to him.
7. Trying to describe verbally when a visual would help him understand.
8. Not applying the subject matter to him and his.

Check your own span of attention in the next meeting you attend. How long can you listen before you notice your chair is uncomfortable, or that the air in the room is getting fogged up with smoke, or you see a secretary in a window across the street? When such things attract your attention away from the speaker, your span of attention has run out. Using PAYOFF speech, the speaker does something to get back your attention.

7. SHOW THAT YOU LIKE HIM

It helps in working with him. You don't have to go as far as sending valentines to him. A salesman I was working with saw a Pittsburgh Pirate cap in a show window in Pittsburgh. He went into the store and bought the cap.

I asked, "Going to take it home to your boy?"

"No, I'm sending it to Fatso in our shipping department. He's a Pirate nut."

I'm sure that the act did not delay the salesman's shipments. But it showed that the salesman liked the man. Will Rogers said, "I never met a man I didn't like." And though Will conversed with all types, they understood him and laughed at his quips, even when they were the butt of his jokes. You listen to the man who seems to like you. Consider the group at your office. You have no trouble conversing with the ones in your football pool or the gang that matches for the Cokes. They understand you and work with you. Then there are some who don't seem to fit in. You can't determine whether or not they are with you or against you. Aren't you more careful in what you say to them?

In social situations it is much the same. You meet a man for the first time and you spar with questions to see what interests you have in common. When you find that he went to Central High School when you were at Taft, you have something to start with. By collecting such bits of information, you get a better picture of his interests, he gets a better picture of yours, you talk and he listens, he talks and you listen, for you have begun to like one another. You can't like everybody, of course, but don't waste time disliking anybody. Your dislike can't help showing through.

One young executive told me that he didn't like the vice-president of his company, and was ill at ease in his presence, yet every month he had to go to the vice-president's office and make a verbal report. "It's the toughest job I have to do," he said. Due to his anxiety his reports were stiff and formal. And what did the vice-president think—that he frightened the young man? No, the executive felt that he was regular, that nobody should be afraid of him. He assumed that the nervous young man was covering up something. Check the men you like in your company. It is easier to do business with them, isn't it?

One of the biggest difficulties in collective bargaining is that the managers hate the union stewards and the union stewards hate the managers. They start any discussion with two strikes against its success.

Like the other fellow and it will be easier to get your message across to him.

8. LET HIM LIKE YOU

This too is a great help. Even a so and-so can be a nice guy when he wants something from you. Think of the wolf who wanted to eat

Red Riding Hood, What you say will PAY OFF better if the listener likes you and thinks you are a good guy. I ask listeners in audiences if they have a TV announcer they don't like. Always a number of hands go up. You probably have one you don't like. You say, "He couldn't sell me anything." Watch that man the next time he does a commercial and try to figure out why you feel that way about him. Do you get the impression that he feels he is speaking to a group of dumb peasants? Study him and try to analyze why you don't like him. Write a list of his faults in your notebook. Study them and, if you have any of the habits you dislike in him, shed them.

Why Others Won't Like You

1. You talk too much.
2. You seem to know it all.
3. You use the capital "I" too much.
4. You throw your weight around.
5. You don't listen courteously.
6. You are rude to others.
7. You interrupt others.
8. You show you feel some of your associates are not your equals.
9. You laugh at others' suggestions.
10. You speak slightingly about others' efforts.
11. You hog credit for the work of employees.
12. You brag about your possessions.

You don't like others with these faults, do you? OK, if you have any of them, correct them. Note how the big mouth of the man you don't like contributes to all of your dislikes. You may feel you are important, but remember others want to feel important too. You make no friends when you state, "I put him in his place." Maybe you did, but telling about your victory doesn't help your image. It doesn't help to mention your two Cadillacs or the million dollars you made. Do you like others who talk to impress you?

Why It Pays to Be Liked

1. Your employees work harder for you, and so you make a better work record.
2. Your superiors will consider you more favorably. If two men are up for promotion, the reputation "everybody likes him" is a help.
3. You make more progress socially.

Don't protest, "Life's not a popularity contest." Popularity helps. Wouldn't that TV announcer you don't like have a better chance of inducing you to try his wares if you liked him?

The good guy doesn't always lose. Not in PAYOFF speech, he doesn't.

9. LISTEN TO HIM

This is the mark of the "good guy." Nothing can make more friends than the ability to listen courteously to others. There is an old saying, "He's my friend, he listens to me." When you are inclined to listen to others, they feel the same about listening to you.

Do You Have Any of These Faults in Listening to Your Employees?

In my speech clinic I ask the men to tell me what irritating habits their bosses have when the men are talking. Here is the list they made up. Do you have any of these faults?

1. He moves papers on his desk.
2. He tries to read a letter.
3. He calls a question to his secretary.
4. He looks up a telephone number.
5. He tries to light a pipe, cigarette, or cigar.
6. He looks out the window and asks a question about what he sees.
7. He makes a note.

8. He opens a desk drawer and looks for something inside it.

9. He works on his fingernails.

10. He tries to get a gravy spot off his tie.

While he is off on any one of these diversions, he may say, "Keep talking, I'm listening." If you have any of these faults forget them. The employee has an idea he wants to present or a question he wants answered. Give him full attention and you'll get a higher rating from him.

Follow This Formula for Listening

Books have been written on the art of listening. Most of us can learn by studying the books. Here is a simple plan that will convince the speaker you are listening:

1. *Look at the speaker*, not at objects on your desk. Try listening with your eyes. Keep your right eye on his right eye.

2. *Hear what is said.* If his story is not clear, ask him questions about it.

3. *Let him know you have heard.* A question or two will help in this, but don't make your questions an interruption.

4. *Show interest*—again questions will help.

Try This Idea

Write the formula for listening on a small card and place it under the glass on your desk. The next time an employee speaks to you, check your performance with the card.

USE THESE IDEAS TO MAKE YOUR SPEECH PAY OFF

Every fault mentioned in this chapter can be corrected easily if you will put these ideas to work:

1. *Understand Your Listener.* He is unusual. There is not another like him. If you know something about his interest and use what you know, your speech will have more appeal to him.

2. *Get His Favorable Attention.* If possible, tell him how he benefits in your first sentence.

3. *Help Him Hear What You Say.* Watch the speed with which you speak, the care you use in enunciation, your clarity. He expects your help in these matters. Give it to him.

4. *Make It Easier for Him to Understand.* Forget the words of doubtful meaning that one of my friends calls "Intellectual Exhibitionism." Anatole France said, "The finest words are only vain words if you cannot understand them."

5. *Arouse His Interest.* The listener is always asking, "What do I get out of this?" Try to show *his* interest in everything you say.

6. *Hold His Interest.* Think of his listening problems. He listens faster than you can speak and he can listen for only so long. Consider these problems in speaking with him. Hold his interest by using devices such as visuals, demonstrations, humor, stories, gossip, news, names.

7. *Show That You Like Him.* If your manner shows you think the listener is beneath you, you'll get little cooperation from him. Show that you feel he is important and he will be glad to work with you.

8. *Let Him Like You.* Your listener will like you if you demonstrate to him that you know what you want and ask for it in the right way.

9. *Listen to Him.* Give him your full attention. You make him feel more important when you listen courteously to what he has to say.

How to Get Instant and Willing Cooperation from Anyone*

3

Just as water cannot rise above its source, we cannot enlighten anyone beyond our own understanding. If we are honest with ourselves, we all shall admit that too often we start speaking without being sure what it is we want to say. I'm sure we all realize that this is a fatal error.

KNOW WHAT YOU WANT TO SAY

Form the habit of taking time to see in your mind's eye a clear and articulate picture of what you desire to communicate before speaking or writing. The importance of the information you desire to communicate and the urgency of the situation will determine how much time you can take for this "mental picture," of course.

This thinking and planning can vary from a casual conversation to hours or even days of outlining, writing and rewriting a speech or presentation of major importance. Remember, an advertising agency may take weeks preparing an important ad containing one picture and a few words to communicate a simple idea to the public. Preliminary thinking and planning is a *must* to avoid communication breakdowns.

---

*Merlyn Cundiff, Kinesics: *The Power of Silent Command* (West Nyack, N.Y.: Parker Publishing Company, Inc., 1972).

Say It in a Way that Can Be Understood

In this chapter we will refer to the one with whom you are trying to communicate as the *respondent*. In various circumstances, your respondent may be an individual, a group, or even an entire audience of hundreds of people. However, this cardinal principle will always apply: Until you have put yourself in your respondent's shoes and adjusted your approach to *his* understanding, not yours, you are not communicating at all. You are only talking to yourself. Remember this corny old adage: Communication is a dance—and it takes two to tango. As you plan what you are going to say, never forget that your very purpose is to persuade and convince the other person. Concentrate on him rather than on yourself. Put yourself in his shoes.

People are not persuaded by what we say but rather by what they understand. In the art of persuasion, if we could only remember that principle, many of the misunderstandings in life could be avoided.

I am sure no one would take issue with the above statement. So let's look at some of the ways of insuring that what is said is related to the respondent's understanding.

FIRST CONSIDER THE RESPONDENT

You certainly would not think you could convey a message to a blind man through the use of sign language. I am sure you would not attempt to engage in oral conversation with a totally deaf person. The utter futility of talking to a person in a language foreign to his would certainly be obvious.

Yet, every day many of us make a communication mistake almost as unforgivable. We use words, phrases and sentences which are not understandable to the person with whom we are talking.

Something we understand today could easily have an entirely different meaning tomorrow because of change in customs or habits. For instance, I heard a girl say the other day that she had a hole in the seat of her stockings. Before the advent of the panty hose this statement would have had no meaning. But I assure you today it is a calculated hazard to any girl's wardrobe.

Watch Your Semantics

A friend of mine, Cavett Robert, recently told me that he took one of his twin daughters to the orthodontist to have her teeth examined.

The dentist took a look at her teeth, frowned, turned to my friend and said, "Your daughter has a traumatic malocclusion."

My friend said that he almost fainted. He thought he was going to lose his little girl.

Why couldn't the orthodontist have used laymen's language and merely said, "Your little girl has a slight over-bite"?

It is unfortunate that the more versed we become in the semantics of our own business or profession the more careful we must be in talking about our business or profession with outsiders. We forget that others are not as familiar with these terms as we are; consequently we are prone to use them in their presence.

Use His Yardstick of Understanding, Not Yours

I was recently waiting in a reception room for an appointment with a person who was engaged in an extensive farming operation.

To pass the time away I was thumbing through a government magazine on raising lettuce. I chanced to come across this statement, "Temperature is an important factor in the ecological optimum of crop development and the consequent exploitation of water and soil resources."

After reading the sentence several times—even writing it—I gave up on it. When the party I was to see finally came out, I handed him the magazine and asked what the mumbo-jumbo meant. He casually looked at it and said, "It means that if the weather is too hot or too cold the crops have a heck of a time."

I can't believe that the farmers, for whom the bulletin was written, would not have been just as confused by such a statement as I was.

Be sure you are on the same thought pattern with your listener.

We all remember the story of the little boy out on the school playground who said to his friend, "I ain't going."

The teacher, overhearing, walked over to him and said, "Don't say that, Johnny—it is 'I am not going, you are not going, she is not going, we are not going, they are not going'."

Johnny looked up and said, "Hey, Teacher, ain't nobody going?"

Any good communicator uses the yardstick of his respondent's understanding in framing his words, phrases and sentences.

Do Your Homework

When I am asked to speak before any group of people, what do you think is my first step? You are right; I must find out all I can about my audience.

A speech that might get a standing ovation from one audience may be destined to utter failure before another audience. This is a lesson I have learned over the years from some sad experiences that I prefer to forget.

Recently I spoke to a group of telephone employees on a phase of communication. Naturally I could take certain liberties with such an audience that would be fatal in a speech to some other group.

So don't we all agree that first we must do our homework and study our audience to be sure just wherein lies the responsive note? This applies to both individuals and groups.

How to Be Flexible in Your Approach

Not long ago I jointly conducted a seminar on Human Engineering with an associate of mine. We were calling on people of varied professions and businesses to secure registrations.

My associate had over the years made such a habit of putting himself in the other person's shoes that without realizing it he would adapt the vernacular of the person on whom we were calling.

To a doctor he might say, "This course will certainly help to *heal* any communication faults you may have."

To a lawyer he would say, "John, the help you will get from this seminar will be a *sure verdict* in your favor."

Even to a garage man I remember he said, "Tom, I've got a real *puncture-proof* proposition for you."

Once I accompanied a real estate broker who called on a cotton farmer to sell him an apartment house. When the discussion of mortgage payments came around the broker said, "Bill, how many bales of cotton do you have stacked up outside? Do you know, Bill, three of those bales each year will make the mortgage payments?"

Now Bill understood the worth of that cotton and just how much land, expense and effort it took to produce each bale. The broker immediately received an enthusiastic response.

I sincerely believe that if this broker had been talking with a dairyman he would have quoted the mortgage payments in terms of the milk from a certain number of cows.

Relating to His Understanding Sets Up the Interview

There is a big difference between an appointment and an interview. When we are able to arrange a physical meeting with an individual we have secured an appointment. However, not until we have gotten into his mental and emotional presence do we have an interview.

Don't confine the application of this principle exclusively to the sales field. It applies in all cases where we deal with people. It is one of the cardinal principles in the art of persuasion.

I am sure that it is unnecessary to emphasize the fact that the surest way to move from the physical to the mental presence is by relating the conversation to matters which are in the field of the *listener's* understanding and interest.

HOW TO CONVINCE RATHER THAN IMPRESS

I had occasion to speak to a state real estate association in a neighboring state. At the same convention and on the program was a vice-president of a bank in that state.

I don't doubt that the banker was well versed in financial matters. In fact his credentials were staggering. However, he made no effort to discuss problems from the real estate person's point of view. Everything he presented was from the approach of a banker and he even used the banker's vernacular. Except for the fact that I was sure I was at a real estate convention, his speech would have made me feel that I was at a bankers' seminar.

When the time came for questions the silence was deafening. The speaker had not only failed to give any solutions but he had not even stimulated or provoked any questions.

It was very obvious that this speaker was so concerned with preserving his banking image that there was no rapport whatsoever with his audience. I am sure you have had occasion to sit in an audience and observe a similar fiasco caused by a speaker.

How to Win Instant Acceptance

At this same convention was another banker. The difference in the reception of the two men was embarrassing. This second banker started out in a simple down-to-earth fashion, carefully relating to the real estate person's problem at the outset.

As I recall, he made an initial statement something like this: "Fellows, I realize you've got problems, serious problems, and I want you to know that we too are concerned over them. The fact is, your problems are our problems and we want to work with you in finding a solution to them."

So many questions evolved that there was time for only about half of them to be discussed.

Go Over to His Side

Talking in terms of the other person's position applies to every facet of life. Child psychologists tell us that nothing is more frustrating to a small child when he is afraid than to be told to "be a big man." In the first place he is not a big man; he is only a child. When we tell him to be a big man, we are trying to bring him over to our world, one which he is not yet prepared by nature to enter.

How much better it would be, psychologists tell us, if we would try to see *his* point of view and go over to *his* world. Why not try to relate to *his* understanding?

Wouldn't Johnny react much better if we said something like this: "Johnny, I know exactly how you feel because when I was your age I felt exactly the same way. But you know, Johnny, as you grow a little older you'll get over it as I did. In fact you'll look back someday and laugh about it."

Now isn't it obvious that we shall give Johnny more courage and that we shall establish better communication with him when we approach the problem from *his* point of view—not ours?

The Need for Understanding Continues

Johnny goes off to prep school and is homesick. Do you think Johnny would buy the approach; "You are now a man, Johnny, don't be a sissy. You don't want to be tied to your mother's apron strings all your life, do you?"

Actually Johnny is still not a man. He is still a boy, a homesick boy, going away from home for the first time. Wouldn't an approach such as this be more effective:

"Johnny, it's tough when anyone who appreciates his home and loves his family has to go away for the first time. It would be sad indeed if your home meant so little to you that you wouldn't go through this experience. All of us go through it and it's bad—I remember. However, Johnny, you'll find that you will make new friends, find new interests, and after a week or two, while you'll not forget your home or love it any less, you'll find that this school will become a second home."

The Need for Understanding on the Job

Johnny has finished college and is in a big corporation that has many employees. At times he is bewildered by company policies and other matters that baffle him.

On one occasion Johnny failed to carry out a directive from his superintendent. The order seemed unnecessary to Johnny. He is now face to face with his superintendent and asks why the order was necessary anyway.

What if the superintendent had been concerned only with preserving his image? What if his major concern had been maintaining his authority? What if he had resorted to the old company policy routine, "Johnny, that is company policy and it's not for you, me or anyone else to question?" Would this have been persuasive communication or even good management? It would have solved nothing, only planted the seed for future trouble.

But let's suppose the superintendent communicates with Johnny by mentally going over to Johnny and mentally stepping into Johnny's shoes: "Johnny, it's very understandable that you should wonder about that order. When I first went with the company I felt just as you do now. In fact, it would be unnatural if every new man didn't feel a little bit as you feel. But you know, Johnny, as time went on and I learned more and more about the workings of the company, I realized that orders of this nature were necessary. Just be patient, Johnny, and go along with us and after a while, you, too, as I did, will realize why it is so important that everyone follows the directives. I'll try to explain to you from time to time why these orders are so vital, although at times they may seem trivial to you."

It wasn't that Johnny really resisted the order, but he had resented the fact that no one had properly communicated with him regarding the purpose of the directives. Now he felt complimented that someone had approached the problem from his point of interest.

How to Bait the Hook

Will Rogers is credited with saying: "When you go fishing you bait the hook, not with what you like, but with what the fish likes. Did you ever taste a worm? Well, it tastes to you perhaps about like your favorite dish tastes to a fish."

A wonderful group of direct salesmen had a convention at Camelback Inn in Scottsdale, Arizona. I spoke at their opening banquet. These were enthusiastic, emotional people—complete extroverts.

My speech was light and entertaining. Purposely I avoided any heavy material. I didn't feel it was necessary to dwell too long on any subject. So I skipped lightly through, enjoying much playback from my audience. Never have I had a speech better received; never have I received more personal satisfaction from speaking.

A week later I spoke in the same room at Camelback, but this time for an engineers' convention. It was a very large convention and there were many people there who were important to my ambitions. In fact there were over 100 heads of companies that put on conventions for their individual companies. I felt sure that I would "wow" this group with the same speech, gaining the same results.

Did You Ever Feel Instant Failure?

Did you ever feel that you were the victim of instant failure? Did you ever suddenly tell yourself that perhaps you were in the wrong line of endeavor?

Those in the audience of engineers who were not looking at me like a tree full of owls had their mental slide-rules measuring my every statement. I felt that I was undergoing the paralysis of analysis.

Yes, I had made the great mistake of not doing my homework. It was the oratorical equivalent of a fumble on the one-yard line. I had neglected to give first consideration to the nature of my audience. I had violated one of the most important rules of good communication. I failed to approach my subject from my audience's point of view.

While a salesman is emotional and thrives on sentiment and generalizations, an engineer is conditioned in his training to analyze carefully, question every statement, and take nothing for granted. While a salesman is easily motivated, an engineer fights against emotion because he feels that it warps his judgment.

Fortunately I had the presence of mind, after seeing my predicament, to reverse my approach. I became more analytical. I used comparisons, examples, testimonials, and offered proof of my position on certain matters.

Although this is not my favorite method of presenting my subject matter, to my relief I gradually saw a radical change in my audience. Before long I almost was convinced that they were rendering a verdict in my favor.

I assure you that this experience was very valuable to me. Never again shall I forget that with an audience as with an individual the communication approach must be made from the other person's point of view. Yes, all we say must be related to the other person's interest and understanding.

FACE SAVING PAYS DIVIDENDS

Sometimes when we fail to relate our conversation to the other person's understanding we put him in a very embarrassing situation.

The average person does not want to indicate that he fails to comprehend for fear he will appear stupid.

Whenever you find that you are attempting to communicate by using words and examples foreign to your listener's understanding you should immediately accept the fact that you are at fault. You should apologize for your inability to make yourself clear. You should convince your listeners that you, and not they, are to blame. One of the worst offenses that you can commit is to attack another person's mental capacity. Whenever you discover that you have directed the conversation into a field where your listener is ill at ease you should save face for him by immediately directing the conversation to another field where he will find himself more comfortable.

How to Use the Nine Memory Power Tactics to Multiply Your Ability to Concentrate*

4

Ben Hogan, one of golfdom's greatest, retired because of "age" and "my inability to concentrate on my game."

Ability to concentrate? Isn't this the stock-in-trade of the scholarly ilk—doctors, lawyers, historians?

It is, but not exclusively. Psychologists tell us now that the ability to concentrate (pay close mental attention to one activity to the exclusion of others) is important in just about any pursuit. Samuel Johnson summed up the role of concentration in memory when he said, "The art of memory is the art of attention." There's probably not much difference in the average person's *ability* to concentrate. There is, however, frequently a big gap in *capability*, due mainly to the manner in which the more efficient go about this cerebral activity.

If you lack the ability to concentrate well, you may find solace in the belief that this is a God-given talent of the chosen. Unfortunately, many people do believe this, and so deprive themselves of what is probably the most important attribute of an efficient memory—the ability to focus attention.

You must, in effect, train yourself in a routine manner to pay close attention in every learning situation, then you will be on your way to that coveted instant memory. Actually, how well you do con-

---

*David V. Lewis, *The Miracle of Instant Memory Power* (West Nyack, N.Y.: Parker Publishing Company, Inc., 1973).

centrate probably depends as much on your mental habits as it does on your intellect. Listed here are some of the methods suggested by leading psychologists for closer concentration:

1. ELIMINATING DISTRACTIONS

In World War II, aircraft executives found that production increased sharply and safety records improved when sweater girls were barred from the assembly line.

An office manager of a big insurance company discovered that placing extra-thick pads under typewriters cut down the high noise factor in his office. Result: more efficient typists and executives.

A promising writer said he made great progress for the first time last year. But only after he had summoned up enough will power to turn off the television set.

All of these things—the sweater girls, noisy typewriters, and the television set—were distractions. They kept people from paying attention to their work. Like many external distractions, they could be eliminated simply by shutting them out.

Some methods are subtler. For example, the employees of a small factory at first got a big kick out of the many THINK signs the "old man" had placed around the plant. But as it turned out, the boss knew what he was doing. "I find," he said, "that when people see enough of these signs, they finally get the idea that people really are thinking. They realize that loud talk and concentration don't go together, so they keep conversation down."

2. SHELVING YOUR PROBLEMS

Inner distractions are infinitely more mysterious. Most of the time we don't know where they come from or why. They may be perfunctory in nature, like the sudden thought of an undone chore. Or, as is often the case, they are serious, like gnawing anxiety over health or financial problems.

A lady fashion editor, admittedly slightly neurotic, used to have a hard time "keeping my head in the game." But not since she learned to keep a "box score" of her problems. When she caught her mind wandering, she would ask herself, "Now just what caused me to lose my chain of thought?"

"I would jot down my answers in the back of my memo pad. Then at the end of the week, I'd analyze the answers. It usually didn't take a psychiatrist to tell me what my problem was."

"Discovering the problem," she adds, "was often the solution itself. But if the problem couldn't be solved right away, I just put it on the shelf. Then I'd have a go at it later."

3. GETTING SET TO LISTEN

Many times, we fail to listen to a speaker simply because we aren't *ready* to pay attention. This state of readiness is a *mental set*. It means that to pay full attention, you must get ready, both physically and mentally, to receive an idea or impression.

There probably never will be a cure-all for the boring speaker. But by assuming the proper mental set, you can do much to get the most from even the most tedious talker.

"I used to attend lots of outside lectures—most of them pretty uninteresting," an ex-teacher says. "Then I found that I was able to get something out of even the dullest lecture by getting myself in the right frame of mind."

Before a meeting, she would find out everything she could about the speaker—his education, work, interests, and so forth. If possible, she'd bone up on the subject, too. "By being reasonably familiar with the subject and the speaker," she says, "I am able to think ahead, draw conclusions, even second-guess the speaker. This makes the talk more interesting. And it's easy to pay attention to—and remember—something you're interested in."

The average speaker gives you abundant opportunity to go through these mental gymnastics. He talks at a rate of 120 to 180 words a minute, authorities say, while the average listener can understand the message at rates of up to 800 words a minute, and in some cases possibly more.

This means that during most talks, you'll have plenty of time to idle your mental motor. It is usually during these lulls that your fancy roams.

Another tip: look directly at the speaker when he's speaking.

Close visual attention contributes to concentrated listening. It is quite difficult to look at another object and actually hear what the speaker has to say.

Learning to listen attentively is still another *must* in developing an instant memory. The super-salesman is not necessarily the best talker, but almost invariably, the best listener—thus, he is likely to remember more.

4. READING RAPIDLY

A successful lawyer told me he often had a difficult time paying attention while reading "nonlegal material." "How rapidly do you read?" I asked. He replied that in his business he had to read everything slowly and "really concentrate."

We generally agree that most of his legal reading could be classified as difficult, requiring a relatively slow reading rate. But the lawyer did concede the possibility that other types of reading could be done at a faster pace.

He enrolled in an executive speed-reading course. A few months later, he found himself racing through newspaper and magazine columns at 700 to 800 words a minute—and often faster—with little if any loss in comprehension. "Reading at this rate," he said, "you hardly have time to do anything other than concentrate on the subject at hand."

Surprisingly, reading experts have found that needlessly slow reading is perhaps the chief cause for wool-gathering while reading. And daydreaming is the nemesis of concentration.

The proper mental set is also important to concentration while reading. This involves reading with a purpose, resting at intervals, and reading selectively.

Thus another milestone you must pass on your way to an instant memory is the ability to read rapidly, when appropriate, and well.

5. SCHEDULING YOUR TIME

A personnel manager of a large department store claims he gets "perpetual energy" by judiciously scheduling his work.

"I always try to keep three or four projects going at the same time," he says. "When I get tired of one, I go to another. I also try to alternate a hard job with an easy one, or a pleasant one with a less desirable one. Much of the fatigue we feel in everyday work is actually boredom. And one of the best ways to fight boredom is to change activities."

His scheduling further entails setting up his most difficult or least-liked chores for his high-energy periods in the day. Conversely, he slates the easy tasks (usually those he is more interested in) for the low-energy periods.

Regardless of the daily schedule, this busy executive finds that occasional breaks can often revive interest and stimulate greater concentration. The 10-minute coffee break is a well-conceived idea. One psychologist proved that most recovery from fatigue resulting from mental work happened in the first 10 minutes of rest.

6. WORKING RAPIDLY

A sales executive who travels a great deal admitted that he literally hated to tackle the backlog of paper work which stacked up while he was away on business trips.

The paper work was not large by any standard, but it was indeed an awesome sight to him. He would spend hours wading through the task—fuming, fretting, and procrastinating—everything that a person who isn't interested does when staving off an unpleasant chore.

Now he does the same work in half the time, and with infinitely less fuss. How? "By diving into it and working like the devil," he boasts. "The faster I work, the more efficiently I seem to be able to do the paper work. In fact, I work so fast that I scarcely have time to think of how unpleasant the job really is."

He never reached the point of "liking" the periodic paper work. But his confidence in his ability to wade through it rapidly was greatly enhanced. The advantage is obvious—same time, save money.

7. BREAKING THE JOB DOWN

The 90-pound weakling is habitually depicted as wanting to "whittle the big beach bully down to his size." Unfortunately, the size of the bully often makes the idea impractical.

Many of us have this same feeling when we are confronted with a formidable business chore. But, in many cases, we *can* whittle the chore down. The idea is to break the job down into smaller, more meaningful parts.

A professor-author I know practices this idea when tackling a tome of some length. "By writing the book a chapter at a time," he says, "I find it much easier to concentrate on one aspect of the overall subject. Then, in the end, I have only the mopping-up operation; you know, tying the loose ends together."

The same idea can often be applied to many workaday chores. You can concentrate more effectively on part of a task because it's simpler.

8. TAKING ACTION

We don't often consider the "thinking man" a man of action. Rodin's *The Thinker* is supposed to be the true picture of a man deep in thought—solemn, brow wrinkled, chin thoughtfully resting on the hand.

Nonsense, say modern psychologists. The person who is really paying attention is more often than not doing it effortlessly. His thoughts flow freely and easily. The wrinkled brow and pained expression usually signal the warm-up period, which comes before true concentration.

"My secretary told me that I pace the floor like a wounded lion when dictating," one executive says. "So I tried to dictate from my swivel chair. The results were nearly disastrous. In the sitting position, my mind went blank. But once I got back into action, the ideas seemed to flow freely."

You do not have to look far, either, to find a speaker who depends on gestures to get his ideas across. These actions actually help him to think. "Tie his hands and he'd be speechless," is the customary gibe thrown his way.

Still others swing a leg, tap a pencil, or drum fingers on a table—all for the sake of pure concentration. However, this may not be the best way to win friends and influence your boss.

9. EXERCISING YOUR MIND

Can you improve your ability to concentrate by "practicing"? Many say you can.

"I practice concentration by trying to pay strict attention to a different subject every day," one sales executive says. "I think about the subject from every possible angle, seeing it in as many lights as possible. Having done this for some months, I find that I can concentrate intensely for from 10 to 30 minutes on just about any subject I choose."

If this feat appears overly simple, try this easy one: Close your eyes and count to 100, visualizing each number as you go. You're above average if you can go the route without letting an outside thought slip in.

Walter B. Pitkin, former Columbia University journalism professor and author, used several similar "exercises" which he claimed helped improve his power to pay attention.

Among other routines, he would play a phonograph record while studying something fairly difficult. When the tune ended, he'd recite aloud to himself what he had been studying. He said this forced him to "blot out sounds to such a degree that I became virtually deaf to them."

There are many other such exercises. One of the more popular ones is to work out a not-too-easy math problem in your head.

Just for fun, why don't you try a few of these attention exercises along with your daily push-ups? And while you're at it, give serious thought to some of the concentration techniques used by others.

Perhaps there is no more single important step in developing your instant memory power than to train yourself to concentrate effectively, even under adverse conditions.

The person with an average memory concentrates well enough, but it is the person who learns to heighten this ability who develops a truly powerful instant memory.

How to Multiply Your Impact on People and Be Master of Every Situation*

5

In order to strengthen your impact on people, you must determine your current impact, learn techniques to project an effective image and then practice those techniques. In this chapter you will, first, see how to evaluate your impact on others by observing their reactions to you.

You can improve your "impact quotient" by following a few simple steps that will enhance your image in the minds of other people. In this chapter you'll learn how to use words, actions, methods and emotions that translate into a positive psychological impact on people.

In this chapter you'll also see how to use the power of your "psychological impact" to improve cooperation from those with whom you interact in your daily life. These principles have been tested in hundreds of business situations and found successful. They have been used by parents in dealing with children and by husbands and wives. They work, and you can use them in your everyday conversations and activities.

---

*Les Donaldson, *How to Use Psychological Leverage to Double the Power of What You Say* (West Nyack, N.Y.: Parker Publishing Company, Inc., 1978).

FOUR WAYS TO MEASURE YOUR "IMPACT QUOTIENT"

You can use one or both of the following techniques to determine your current impact on others.

Seek Feedback to Measure Your Impact

The most obvious way to get feedback is to ask for it. Ask someone you work with to evaluate your impact on others. Ask him to listen to a conversation between you and a subordinate or peer and then give you his opinion on the impact you had on the other person. He may report, after the listening session, that you were too easy or too harsh. He may point out specific places where the things you say are working against the objectives you are trying to accomplish.

I used this procedure once during a review session with a product department head. The department head had consistently refused to follow my instructions in the handling of direct sales. My instructions were that the shipment was to go from the manufacturing plant directly to the purchaser without intervening storage.

I asked a peer to sit in as a critical observer, while I reviewed this subordinate's performance. The peer was to listen carefully and try to determine the impact my remarks made on the subordinate. He would discuss his observations with me privately after the review meeting was concluded.

During the review, I tried to listen to the reasons the product manager gave for not following my instructions. Often he had sales, he said, that did not fill the truck. He had to fill the truck in order to get the lowest freight rate. In order to fill the truck, he would purchase product that was not sold and upon arrival, place the unsold product in storage in a public warehouse. I told him I understood the problem of filling the truck, but insisted that in the future he must avoid storing product in public storage.

After the review my critical observer gave me his impression. He pointed out that I had a negative impact upon the subordinate. He doubted that the problem had been solved at all. I had, in his opinion, left an impression that I was only interested in getting my own way. He felt I had missed an opportunity to explore the costs involved in the storage system, and he believed that by comparing costs of the two systems I could have gained understanding and commitment from the subordinate.

Use the "Question-Response" Yardstick

Another way to seek feedback is to specifically ask the person you are dealing with. When discussing a problem with a subordinate, you can say: "What do you think?", "How will that work?", "Will what I've said cause you any problems?", "What obstacles do you see?, "Is there any problem with what I've said?"

Many people are reluctant to tell you that you are having a negative impact upon them. But most people will, when asked, give you their opinion on problems or obstacles that you are introducing. You can analyze those responses to determine your impact quotient.

Use the "Nonverbal Observation" Yardstick

You can also learn a great deal about your impact by watching and listening to others. If the other person responds warmly and enthusiastically, you may assume your impact to be positive. If the other person seems to be reluctant to talk, if he grimaces, makes subtle objections or is openly argumentative, you will know your impact is negative. It may develop that there are other reasons for these reactions, but generally they are influenced by your behavior.

The mere fact that you start observing other people's nonverbal behavior will help you strengthen your impact. If you watch closely, you will detect irritation, nervousness, preoccupation, and lack of commitment. The longer you observe, the more aware you will become of the subtle clues people give to indicate their feelings.

Once aware of these clues, you can direct comments and questions to the problem area. Let's suppose a manager is talking to a foreman. He is telling the foreman he needs overtime worked to meet the production budget. He notices the foreman's face drop. He seems to be provoked at having to work overtime. The manager asks questions and finds the foreman has a personal problem that needs immediate attention. If the manager had not been watching nonverbal behavior, if he had not been seeking feedback, he might have missed the clue. He would then have missed the opportunity to improve his impact on the foreman.

Evaluate Your "Cooperation Index"

When you ask your subordinates to work overtime or to increase production to meet a deadline, you have an opportunity to check your impact quotient. If you get the increased production, your impact is positive; if not, it may indicate a negative impact. The willingness of your subordinates to cooperate is a valuable indication of your impact on others.

You can evaluate the cooperation of your peers as another indication of your impact quotient. If your peers are constantly finding excuses not to give you needed help, this may indicate a reluctance to cooperate with you. If your requests are often denied, even when you can see that there is no reason for their denial, this strongly implies a negative impact.

You can also evaluate your relationship with your superiors. If you are given the necessary support you require to carry out your assignments, this cooperation indicates a positive impact. If your superiors cooperate by approving your recommendations, providing financial or other support, your impact quotient is obviously positive.

You may also get an indication of your impact on people by evaluating the cooperation you get from your family, friends and neighbors. Form the habit of evaluating the cooperation you get from people to determine your "impact quotient."

THREE WAYS TO IMPROVE YOUR "IMPACT QUOTIENT"

You can improve your impact on others. You can break through defensiveness, rationalization, multiple objections, inattention, aggressiveness and unresponsiveness. You can gain control in conversation, develop cooperation from others and build morale by using in everyday situations techniques developed by psychologists for professional counselling.

How to Use the "Discussion-Time-Phase" Technique to Gain Control

Often in conversation, we find that understanding is blocked due to the defensiveness or aggressiveness expressed by subordinates.

Others may constantly veer away from the purpose of the conversation or fail to respond in a constructive way. You can gain control when confronted with these non-productive behaviors by using the "Discussion-Time-Phase" technique.

The "time-phase" is a pause to permit the other person time to absorb your comments, freedom to respond to each comment separately and the freedom to express his feelings as well as his ideas. The "Discussion-Time-Phase" technique builds an obligation on the part of the other person to listen open-mindedly to you. Your behavior, over time, will have such an impact on the other person as to influence him to actually copy your behavior. This leads to understanding.

The first technique then, for improving your impact on others, is simply to *pause after you make a comment, to give the other time to absorb what you have said.* If your comment is a new or novel idea, a longer pause will be required. The more complex the comment the more time the other will need to absorb and integrate the idea into his own mind.

A study conducted by the U.S. Navy showed that when a lecturer provided pauses, the participants remembered 58 percent of the material. Groups given the lectures without pauses under the same conditions, remembered only 37 percent of the material. The groups which were given pauses utilized the time to do something with the new material. They took notes or thought about the content; they integrated it into their own thinking.

In conversation you can do the same thing the Navy did. You can allow time for subordinates or others to integrate or do something with your comments. Even though they will not always accept them, if given time to think about them, they may understand them.

How to Use "Transitional Questioning" to Control the Conversation

A second technique for strengthening your impact on others is to employ "Transitional Questioning" to control the conversation. There are three main categories of questions, each of which accomplishes a different purpose: The three categories are convergent, divergent and evaluative.

1. Convergent questions pull the conversation toward a specific point.

2. Divergent questions pull the conversation toward a general area.
3. Evaluative questions open the conversation to feelings and opinions.

Convergent questions draw the other's thinking toward a specific conclusion. They are used to pull bits of information from a wide background and collate these bits as they relate to a specific topic. Convergent questions bring the facts from various sources together in the formation of a pattern or a conclusion. For example, we might draw out through questioning, legal, moral, religious and economic principles that relate to unemployment. We would then converge these principles into a proposal for dealing with unemployment.

Divergent questions are used to get the same result as convergent questions; but they are used to lead the other from a specific conclusion to a generalization. This generalization is then shown to cover the problem of current concern. Divergent questions direct the interpretation or the translation from the generalized whole or pattern to a specific application.

Evaluative questions, the third category, are the most useful in two-way discussion. Evaluative questions give the other person the freedom to state his opinions. With those opinions often come feelings, doubts and concerns which provide the basis for discussion that will lead to understanding.

You can pre-plan questions that will improve your impact on your subordinates in every interaction. You can initiate, guide and direct the course of the conversation with these "Transitional Questions." You can elicit information that will simplify getting the job done, deciding between alternatives and making decisions.

Questioning not only gives you control over the conversation, it gives you the understanding necessary to make better decisions. In *New Patterns of Management*, Rensis Likert (1961) reported that 95 percent of the foremen questioned in his study thought they understood their men's problems well. In answering the same question, 66 percent of the subordinates said the foremen did not understand. Questioning will resolve this problem.

A thorough understanding of the situation cannot be accomplished with one question. You need to ask questions to determine the facts and ask for reasons to explain the facts. Then you ask for the feelings or opinions of the subordinate or other person about the situation. You might first ask, "What is the problem?" then, "What caused this?" or "Why is it a problem?" and then ask, "How do you feel about this problem?" or "What is your opinion of the problem?" These questions will provide a background of information that will give you the understanding that many subordinates say management doesn't have.

Questioning techniques work well because people generally provide answers to protect their own image of themselves. Many people have an ego-related fear that if they don't know some bit of information, they will be thought of as "not in on what's going on." Others fear being thought secretive or deceitful. People also have a biological drive to complete each situation. For these three reasons, people will generally give you the answers you need, especially if you explain why you need the information.

How to Time Your Presentation for Maximum Impact

A third technique in strengthening your impact through two-way discussion is to *time the presentation of your comments or opinions to coincide with a receptive period of the subordinate or other person.* As discussed previously, the other person will show this receptivity by asking questions, expressing doubts or showing some form of approval.*

Psychologists tell us that people tend not to hear clearly enough to understand or remember messages with which they disagree. If the other person expresses any disagreement, then you are facing a more difficult task. The best approach is, after thorough questioning, to build up a receptive state, to solicit the other's opinion on each comment you make. This will help make sure he understands what you have said.

You will be able to gain commitment to your decisions if you can develop this understanding. Even if the subordinate disagrees with your decision, if he understands your reasons and your goals, he will be more likely to do what you want. This understanding creates an

---

*V.R. Buzzota, Ph.D., R.E. Lefton, Ph.D., and Manuel Sherberg, *Effective Selling Through Psychology: Dimensional Sales and Sales Management Strategies.* (New York; Wiley Interscience, 1972), p. 204.

obligation to follow your instructions and eliminates the possibility of excuses due to a lack of understanding.

FOUR WAYS TO USE YOUR "PSYCHOLOGICAL IMPACT" TO IMPROVE COOPERATION FROM PEOPLE

You can get better results, increase the power of your words, expand your influence and gain cooperation from people by using your "Psychological Impact" in a constructive way. "Active Listening," "Feedback Contingency," "Monitored Freedom" and "Environmental Monitoring" are four techniques that you can use to develop cooperation from others.

The Principles and Techniques of "Active Listening"

The basic technique used by Dr. Rogers to gain cooperation from others was *active listening*. Dr. Rogers (1957) found that people who were listened to carefully and sensitively began to clarify their own thoughts and attempted to present them more clearly. The fact that someone really cared about what they had to say caused them to think carefully when speaking.

Since there was no threat or criticism, people who were listened to began to open up more, became more cooperative and began to follow the example set by the listener. And they began to listen more themselves.

You can use active listening to gain cooperation from your subordinates, peers and superiors. The basic success of active listening is due to its orientation toward the other person. When you listen carefully to another person you are showing respect for that person. You are also showing concern for him. One way to show that you have listened to a person is to relate back to something this person has said in the past.

You might start your program of active listening by listening for some specific thing that seems important to the other person. Make a mental note of this and then you can question or comment on it from time to time to show the other person you are concerned enough about his problems to remember them.

The purpose of active listening is to remove barriers that cause defensiveness in others; to provide psychological safety for others; to encourage them to express their feelings and opinions openly; to encourage them to listen to and evaluate others' ideas; and to encourage their cooperation.

Active listening requires that we avoid passing judgment. The avoidance of criticism will provide the atmosphere conducive to cooperation. If there is no criticism there is no reason for defensiveness or argumentativeness.

The following steps, based on Dr. Rogers' recommendations, have been developed and tested in business and social situations. These nine steps, after extensive testing, have been revised and made applicable to all situations. Cooperation can be gained by managers from their subordinates, by salesmen from their customers, by parents from their children or by anyone who practices the nine steps in his everyday activities.

Nine Steps for Active Listening to Get Cooperation from Everyone

1. Listen for clues to emotional distractions as well as comments relevant to the discussion.
2. Respond to the emotion by using reflective statements or probes. Let the other person know that you accept and understand his feelings.
3. Show you are listening by responding to irrelevant remarks.
4. Listen carefully, without interrupting, to show respect for the other person's ideas and opinions.
5. Watch for nonverbal clues to determine the other person's level of receptivity.
6. Test for understanding by using summary statements and asking questions to clarify the other's position. The use of summary statements also shows respect. It shows you respect the other enough to pay attention to what he says.
7. Express your own feelings freely and genuinely when the other person is receptive. Be honest in your opinion even though it may clash with the opinion of the other person.

8. Pause after you express your opinion, so the other person will have time to evaluate it.

9. If the other person does not respond to your statement, ask a question to determine whether or not he understood your opinion.

Using the "Feedback Contingency" Concept

Whether or not people change their behavior is contingent upon the feedback they get. You can gain more cooperation by providing feedback that shows them the value of cooperation. One way of doing this is to provide a model of cooperative behavior where positive results can be seen. This is one way of using the "Feedback Contingency" concept.

Humans continue into adulthood their childhood practice of patterning their behavior after significant adults. As adults, however, they are more selective in the acquisition of patterns and are more subtle in expressing them. The patterning, however subtle, encompasses all behavior that seems to them to be effective.

The selection of the significant other is related to the success or impact this person has on those with whom he interacts. The most significant behaviors will be assimilated and utilized by those subordinates who see the behavior as successful.

You can gain cooperation from others by demonstrating the usefulness of cooperation. By cooperating with others in plain view of your subordinates, you provide a pattern for them to assimilate into their own behavior.

Providing accurate feedback to subordinates gives them the information necessary for their motivation. It has been proven over and over again that employees at all levels will improve their performance once they become aware that their results are lower than expected.

If you show your subordinates the gap between their actual performance and the goal they are expected to achieve, and then provide daily or weekly feedback, their performance will improve more rapidly than you may think possible.

If you are dealing with production employees, for example, and your goal is 100 units per hour, you must first make the goal known. Then post daily production figures, so that the workers can see the gap between where they are and where they should be. The goal-striving psychology of each of them will motivate them to reach the goal. Unless there are mitigating problems, you should see major improvement within five to six weeks.

Applying the "Monitored Freedom" Concept

A third technique in gaining cooperation from others is to *help them satisfy their physical and ego needs.* Psychologists tell us that the frustration of physical needs results in anger and hostility. The ego needs grow out of this same frustration. The person whose physical needs are frustrated develops the ego-related need for power, freedom, and knowledge which can be used in the satisfaction of the physical needs.

With power and freedom from the dependency of others, physical needs are not likely to be frustrated by others. The primary reason for the development of the ego-needs, then, is to avoid the frustrations resulting from having others block the physical needs.

In the work situation, you can provide this feeling of freedom simply by giving each subordinate an opportunity to speak freely or have the freedom to participate in improving his job. Personal conversations and written suggestions both offer the subordinate the freedom to have an impact on his job. Give him this freedom and make him aware that you are purposely doing it.

A person who realizes that his observations and ideas will be listened to is more likely to be cooperative. His needs for freedom and recognition are being fulfilled. Consequently there is no frustration. When there is no frustration, instead of anger there will be a warmer feeling leading to cooperation.

Using the "Environmental Monitoring" Concept

A fourth technique that insures cooperation is to *provide a predictable environment for your subordinates.* People need to know that they will be treated fairly, receive social and financial rewards for good work and that these conditions will remain stable. No man can please a superior who changes the rules each day. Just as uncertainty breeds resistance, predictability breeds cooperation. Monitor these environmental factors on a regular basis and try to keep the environment predictable.

A TEN-POINT GUIDE TO PRACTICAL APPLICATION

The following ten points offer an effective guideline for developing a highly productive group of subordinates with high morale who will be highly cooperative.

1. Group your subordinate staff and supervisory personnel into three- to seven-man teams. You may have more than seven men on one team depending upon organizational structure or the number of divisions you are dealing with. For example, you might have nine divisions, in which case you would work with the nine division managers as one team.

Never form teams of fewer than three people. Two will, in most situations, not be an effective problem-solving team. Leave production personnel in complete production units regardless of the number. Salesmen should be left in groups conforming to their organizational grouping also. A supervisor with more than twelve or fourteen salesmen should consider breaking them into two groups for discussion and problem-solving sessions.

2. Train all management or supervisory personnel to measure and improve their Impact Quotient. They should listen patiently to their employees, not become emotionally involved, provide feedback without criticism, protect the subordinates' dignity, support the employees with advice, help and training, learn the employees' needs and offer guidance that will help them fulfill those needs. Use the Active Listening technique to win their trust and confidence.

3. Develop a high team spirit with each team. Make each team member feel that he is a member of an elite group with special skills, that he is better trained and more highly skilled than his counterparts in other companies.

4. Provide a feedback method to measure their achievements that makes them look good as they progress. Look for positive aspects to emphasize and relate to mistakes as a part of the learning process.

5. Hold team meetings often. Provide for social contact so that the formal and informal organization is the same. Don't expect too much from the first few meetings. In the early stages, many expressions of feelings and irrelevant remarks will be made. Hidden "agendas" will impede progress and work against cooperation. Later, when these feel-

ings have been aired and specific goals have been established, more progress will be made, more cooperation will evolve.

6. Constantly work toward improving working conditions. Try to satisfy as many as possible of the subordinates' physical needs. Increase salary, fringe benefits, and working conditions. Monitor the environment and try to keep it predictable. Apply company policy fairly.

7. Enhance each subordinate's self-image. Ask for his opinions, remember and comment on things that are important to him, let him know you consider him a professional, let him know in every way that his personal dignity and self-esteem are important to you. Practice Active Listening; provide for the freedom of self-expression.

8. Keep communications open in both directions. Provide specific goals and problems for team meetings. Ask for feedback from individual members of each team.

9. Make certain the goals are obtainable. Let the team members participate in goal setting.

10. Make training programs available so that each employee can attain the highest possible level of proficiency.

How to Move Ahead Effortlessly by Thinking like a Leader*

6

Remind yourself frequently that you are not pulled to high levels of success. Rather, you are *lifted* there by those working beside and below you.

Achieving high-level success requires the support and the cooperation of others. And gaining this support and cooperation requires leadership ability. Success and the ability to lead others—that is, getting them to do things they wouldn't do if they were not led—go hand-in-hand.

The success-producing principles explained in this book are valuable equipment in helping you develop your leadership capacity. At this point we want to master four special leadership rules or principles that can cause others to do things for us in the executive suite, in business, in social clubs, in the home, anywhere we find people.

These four leadership rules or principles are:

1. Trade minds with the people you want to influence.
2. Think: What is the human way to handle this?
3. Think progress, believe in progress, push for progress.
4. Take time out to confer with yourself.

---

*David J. Schwartz, *The Magic of Thinking Big* (Englewood Cliffs, N.J.: Prentice-Hall, Inc., 1959).

Practicing these rules produces results. Putting them to use in everyday situations takes the mystery out of that gold-plated word, *leadership*.

LEADERSHIP RULE NUMBER 1:
TRADE MINDS WITH THE PEOPLE YOU WANT TO INFLUENCE

Trading minds with the people you want to influence is a magic way to get others—friends, associates, customers, employees—to act the way you want them to act. Study these two case histories and see why.

Ted B. worked as a television copywriter and director for a large advertising agency. When the agency obtained a new account, a children's shoe manufacturer, Ted was assigned responsibility for developing several TV commercials.

A month or so after the campaign had been launched it became clear that the advertising was doing little or nothing to increase "product movement" in retail outlets. Attention was focused on the TV commercials, because in most cities only television advertising was used.

Through research of television viewers, they found that about 4 per cent of the people thought it was simply a great commercial, "one of the best," these 4 per cent said.

The remaining 96 per cent were either indifferent to the commercials, or in plain language, thought they "smelled." Hundreds of comments like these were volunteered, "It's wacky. The rhythm sounds like a New Orleans Band at 3 A.M." "My kids like to watch most TV commercials but when that shoe thing comes on they go to the bathroom or refrigerator." "I think it's too uppity up." "Seems to me someone's trying to be too clever."

Something especially interesting turned up when all the interviews were put together and analyzed. The 4 per cent that liked the commercial were people pretty much like Ted in terms of income, education, sophistication, and interests. The remaining 96 per cent were definitely in a different "socio-economic" class.

Ted's commercials, which cost almost $20,000, flopped because Ted thought only of his own interests. He had prepared the commercials thinking of the way he buys shoes, not the way the great majority buys shoes. He developed commercials that pleased him *personally*, not commercials that pleased the great bulk of the people.

Results would have been much different had Ted projected himself into the minds of the masses of ordinary people and asked himself two questions: "If I were a parent, what kind of commercial would make me want to buy those shoes?" "If I were a child, what kind of commercial would make me go tell my Mom or Dad that I want those shoes?"

Why Joan Failed in Retailing

Joan is an intelligent, well-educated, and attractive girl of 24. Fresh from college, Joan got a job as an assistant buyer in ready-to-wear goods at a low-to-medium-priced department store. She came highly recommended. "Joan has ambition, talent, and enthusiasm," one letter said. "She is certain to succeed in a big way."

But Joan did not succeed in a "big way." Joan lasted only 8 months and then quit retailing for other work.

I knew her buyer well and one day I asked him what happened.

"Joan is a fine girl and she has many fine qualities," he said. "But she had one major limitation."

"What was that?" I asked.

"Well, Joan was forever buying merchandise that she liked but most of our customers didn't. She selected styles, colors, materials, and prices she liked without putting herself in the shoes of the people who shop here. When I'd suggest to her that maybe a certain line wasn't right for us, she'd say, "Oh, they'll love this. I do. I think this will move fast."

"Joan had been brought up in a well-to-do home. She had been educated to want quality. Price was not important to her. Joan just couldn't see clothing through the eyes of low- to middle-income people. So the merchandise she bought just wasn't suitable."

The point is this: to get others to do what you want them to do you must see things through their eyes. When you trade minds, the secret of how to influence other people effectively shows up. A very successful salesman friend told me he spends a lot of time anticipating how prospects will react to his presentation before he gives it. Trading minds with the audience helps the speaker design a more interesting, harder hitting talk. Trading minds with employees helps the supervisor provide more effective, better received instructions.

A young credit executive explained to me how this technique worked for him.

"When I was brought into this store (a medium-sized clothing store) as assistant credit manager, I was assigned the job of handling all collection correspondence. The collection letters the store had been using greatly disappointed me. They were strong, insulting, and threatening. I read them and thought, 'Brother, I'd be mad as hell if somebody sent me letters like these. I never would pay.' So I just got to work and started writing the kind of letter that would move me to pay an overdue bill if I received it. It worked. By putting myself in the shoes of the overdue customer, so to speak, collections climbed to a record high."

Numerous political candidates lose elections because they fail to look at themselves through the minds of the typical voters. One political candidate for a national office, apparently fully as qualified as his opponent, lost by a tremendous margin for one single reason. He used a vocabulary that only a small per cent of the voters could understand.

His opponent, on the other hand, thought in terms of the voter's interests. When he talked to farmers, he used their language. When he spoke to factory workers, he used words they were easily familiar with. When he spoke on TV, he addressed himself to Mr. Typical Voter, not to Dr. College Professor.

Keep this question in mind, "What would I think of this if I exchanged places with the other person?" It paves the way to more successful action.

Thinking of the interests of the people we want to influence is an excellent rule in every situation. A few years ago a small electronics manufacturer developed a fuse that would never blow out. The manufacturer priced the product to sell for $1.25 and then retained an advertising agency to promote it.

The account executive placed in charge of the advertising immediately became intensely enthusiastic. His plan was to blanket the country with mass advertising on TV, radio, and newspapers. "This is it," he said. "We'll sell 10 million the first year." His advisers tried to caution him, explaining that fuses are not a popular item, they have no romantic appeal, and people want to get by as cheaply as possible when they buy fuses. "Why not," the advisors said, "use selected magazines and sell it to the high income levels?"

They were overruled and the mass campaign was underway only to be called off in six weeks because of "disappointing results."

The trouble was this: the advertising executive looked at the high-priced fuses with his eyes, the eyes of a $30,000-a-year person. He failed to see the product through the eyes of the mass market—the $4000-to-$7000-a-year income levels. Had he put himself in their position, he would have seen the wisdom of directing the promotion toward the upper income groups and the account would have been saved.

Develop your power to trade minds with the people you want to influence. The exercises below will help.

Practice Trading Minds

Exercises

Situation	For Best Results, Ask Yourself
1. Giving someone work instructions	"Looking at this from the viewpoint of someone who is new to this, have I made myself clear?"
2. Writing an advertisement	"If I were a typical prospective buyer, how would I react to this ad?"
3. Telephone manners	"If I were the other person, what would I think of my telephone voice and manners?"
4. Gift	"Is this gift something I would like or is it something he will like?" (Often there is an enormous difference.)
5. The way I give orders	"Would I like to carry out orders if they were given to me the way I give them to others?"
6. Child discipline	"If I were the child—considering his age, experience, and emotions—how would I react to this discipline?"
7. My appearance	"What would I think of my superior if he were dressed like me?"

8. Preparing a speech	"Considering the background and interests of the audience, what would I think of this remark?"
9. Entertainment	"If I were my guests, what kinds of food, music, and entertainment would I like best?"

Put the trading minds principle to work for you:

1. Consider the other person's situation. Put yourself in his shoes, so to speak. Remember, his interests, income, intelligence, and background may differ considerably from yours.

2. Ask yourself, "If I were in his situation, how would I react to this?" (Whatever it is you want him to do.)

3. Take the action that would move you if you were the other person.

LEADERSHIP RULE NUMBER 2—THINK: WHAT IS THE HUMAN WAY TO HANDLE THIS.

People use different approaches to leadership situations. One approach is to assume the position of a dictator. The dictator makes all decisions without consulting those affected. He refuses to hear his subordinates' side of a question because, down deep perhaps, he's afraid the subordinate might be right and this would cause him to lose face.

Dictators don't last long. Employees may fake loyalty for a while, but unrest soon develops. Some of the best employees leave, and those remaining get together and plot against the tyrant. The result is that the organization ceases to function smoothly. This puts the dictator in bad light with his superior.

A second leadership technique is the cold, mechanical, I'm-a-rule-book-operator approach. The fellow using this approach handles everything exactly according to the book. He doesn't recognize that every rule or policy or plan is only a guide for the *usual* cases. This would-be leader treats human beings as machines. And of all things people don't like, perhaps the most disliked is being treated like a machine. The cold, impersonal, efficiency expert is not an ideal. The "machines" that work for him develop only part of their energy.

Persons who rise to tremendous leadership heights use a third approach that we call "Being Human."

Several years ago I worked closely with John S., who is an executive in the engineering development section for a large aluminum manufacturer. John had mastered the "Be Human" approach and was enjoying its rewards. In dozens of little ways John made his actions say, "You are a human being. I respect you. I'm here to help you in every way I can."

When an individual from another city joined his department, John went to considerable personal inconvenience to help him find suitable housing.

Working through his secretary and two other women employees, he set up office birthday parties for each member of the staff. The 30 minutes or so required for this little affair was not a cost; rather, it was an investment in getting loyalty and output.

When he learned that one of his staff members belonged to a minority faith, John called him in and explained that he would arrange for him to observe his religious holidays which don't coincide with the more common holidays.

When an employee or someone in the employee's family was ill, John remembered. He took time to compliment his staff individually for their off-the-job accomplishments.

But the largest evidence of John's "Be Human" philosophy showed up in the way he handled a dismissal problem. One of the employees who had been hired by John's predecessor simply lacked the aptitude and interest for the work involved. John handled the problem magnificently. He did not use the conventional procedure of calling the employee into his office, giving him first the bad news and then second, 15 or 30 days to move out.

Instead, he did two unusual things. First, he explained why it would be to the employee's personal advantage to find a new situation where his aptitudes and interests would be more useful. He worked with the employee and put him in touch with a reputable vocational guidance consultant. Next, he did something else above and beyond the call of duty. He helped the employee find a new job by setting up interviews with executives in other companies where the employee's skills were needed. In just 18 days after the "dismissal" conference the employee was relocated in a very promising situation.

This dismissal procedure intrigued me, so I asked John to explain his thinking behind it. He explained it this way: "There's an old maxim I've formed and held in my mind," he began. "Whoever is under a man's power is under his protection, too. We never should have hired this man in the first place because he's not cut out for this kind of work. But since we did, the least I could do was help him to relocate.

"Anybody," John continued, "can hire a man. But the test of leadership is how one handles the dismissal. Helping that employee relocate before he left us built up a feeling of job security in everyone in my department. I let them know by example that no one gets dumped on the street as long as I'm here."

Make no mistake. John's "Be Human" brand of leadership paid off. There were no secret gossip sessions about John. He received unquestioned loyalty and support. He had maximum job security because he gave maximum job security to his subordinates.

For about 15 years I've been close to a fellow I'll call Bob W. Bob is in his late fifties now. He came up the hard way. With a hit-or-miss sort of education and no money, Bob found himself out of work in 1931. But he's always been a scrambler. Not one to be idle, Bob started an upholstery shop in his garage. Thanks to his untiring efforts, the business grew and today it's a modern furniture manufacturing plant with over 300 employees.

Today Bob is a millionaire. Money and material things have ceased to be a concern. Bob is rich in other ways too. He's a millionaire in friends, contentment, and satisfaction.

Of Bob's many fine qualities, his tremendous desire to help other people stands out. Bob is *human* and he's a specialist in treating others the way human beings want to be treated.

One day Bob and I were discussing the matter of criticizing people. Bob's human way for doing it is a master formula. Here's the way he put it, "I don't think you could find anybody who would say I'm a softie or a weakling. I run a business. When something isn't going right, I fix it, but it's the way I fix it that's important. If employees are doing something wrong or are making a mistake, I am doubly careful not to hurt their feelings and make them feel small or embarrassed. I just use four simple steps.

First, I talk to them privately.

Second, I praise them for what they are doing well.

Third, I point out the one thing at the moment that they could do better and I help them find the way.

Fourth, I praise them again on their good points.

"This four-step formula works. When I do it this way people thank me because I've found that's exactly the way they like it. When they walk out of this office they have been reminded that they are not only pretty good, they can be even better.

"I've been betting on people all my life," Bob says. "And the better I treat them the more good things happen to me. I honestly don't plan it that way. That's just the way it works out.

"Let me give you an example. Back about, oh, five or six years ago, one of the production men came to work drunk. Pretty soon there was a commotion in the plant. It seems this fellow had taken a 5-gallon can of lacquer and was splashing it all over the place. Well, the other workmen took the lacquer away from him, and the plant superintendent escorted him out.

"I walked outside and found him sitting against the building in a kind of stupor. I helped him up, put him in my car and took him to his home. His wife was frantic. I tried to reassure her that everything would be all right. 'Oh, but you don't understand,' she said. 'Mr. W. (me) doesn't stand for anyone being drunk on the job. Jim's lost his job and now what will we do.' I told her Jim wouldn't be dismissed. She asked how I knew. The reason, I explained, is because I'm Mr. W.

"She almost fainted. I told her I'd do all I could to help Jim at the plant and I hoped she'd do all she could at home; and just have him on the job in the morning.

"When I got back to the plant I went down to Jim's department and spoke to Jim's co-workers. I told them 'You've seen something unpleasant here today but I want you to forget it. Jim will be back tomorrow. Be kind to him. He's been a good worker for a long time and we owe it to him to give him another chance.'

"Jim got back on the ball and his drinking was never again a problem. I soon forgot about the incident. But Jim didn't. Two years ago the headquarters of the local union sent some men out here to negotiate the contract for the local. They had some staggering, simply unrealistic demands. Jim—quiet, meek Jim—suddenly became a leader. He got busy and reminded the fellows in the plant that they'd always gotten a fair deal from Mr. W. and we didn't need outsiders coming in to tell us how to run our affairs.

"The outsiders left and as usual we negotiated our contract like friends, thanks to Jim."

Here are two ways to use the "Be Human" approach to make you a better leader. First, each time you face a difficult matter involving people, ask yourself, *"What is the human way to handle this?"*

Ponder over this question when there is disagreement among your subordinates, or when an employee creates a problem.

Remember Bob W's formula for helping others correct their mistakes. Avoid sarcasm. Avoid being cynical. Avoid taking people down a peg or two. Avoid putting others in their place.

Ask, "What is the human way to deal with people?" It always pays—sometimes sooner, sometimes later, but it always pays.

A second way to profit from the "Be-Human" rule is to *let your action show you put people first.* Show interest in your subordinates' off-the-job accomplishments. Treat everyone with dignity. Remind yourself that the primary purpose in life is to enjoy it. As a general rule, the more interest you show in a person, the more he will produce for you. And his production is what carries you forward to greater and greater success.

Praise your subordinates to your supervisor by putting in plugs for them at every opportunity. It's an old American custom to admire the fellow who's on the side of the little man. Your subordinates will appreciate your plugs and their loyalty to you will grow. And do not fear that this will lower your own importance in the eyes of your supervisor. Rather, a man big enough to be humble appears more confident than the insecure man who feels compelled to call attention to his accomplishments. A little modesty goes a long way.

Praise your subordinates personally at every opportunity. Praise them for their cooperation. Praise them for every extra effort they put forth. Praise is the greatest single incentive you can give people, and it costs you nothing. Besides, a "write-in vote" has often overthrown a powerful, known candidate. You never know when your subordinates can do you a turn by coming to your defense.

Practice praising people.

Rub people the *right* way. Be human.

LEADERSHIP RULE NUMBER 3:
THINK PROGRESS, BELIEVE IN PROGRESS, PUSH FOR PROGRESS.

One of the most complimentary things anyone can say about you is, "He stands for progress. He's the man for the job."

Promotions in all fields go to individuals who believe in—and push for—progress. Leaders, real leaders, are in short supply. Status quo-ers (the everything's all-right-let's-don't-upset-the-apple-cart folks) far outnumber the progressives (the there's-lots-of-room- for-improvement-let's-get-to-work-and-do-it-better people). Join the leadership elite. Develop a forward look.

There are two special things you can do to develop your progressive outlook:

1. Think Improvement in Everything You Do.
2. Think High Standards in Everything You Do.

Several months ago the president of a medium-sized company asked me to help him make an important decision. This executive had built the business by himself and had been functioning as sales manager. Now, with seven salesmen employed, he decided his next step was to promote one of his salesmen to the job of sales manager. He narrowed the choice down to three, all of whom were about equal in experience and sales performance.

My assignment was to spend one day in the field with each man and then report my views on which fellow seemed to be best qualified to lead the group. Each man was told that a consultant would visit him to discuss the over-all marketing program. For obvious reasons, they were not told the specific purpose of my visit.

Two of the men reacted pretty much the same way. Both were uncomfortable with me. They seemed to sense that I was there to "change things." Each of these men was a real defender of the status quo. Both approved the way everything was being done. I raised questions about how the territories were laid out, the compensation program, the sales promotional material—every facet of the marketing effort. But on all points, the response was always "Everything is okay." On specific points these two men explained why the present way couldn't and shouldn't be changed. Summed up, both men wanted the status quo to remain the status quo. One of them said to me as he dropped me by my hotel, "I don't know exactly why you spent the day with me, but tell Mr. M. for me that everything is okay as is. Don't go refiguring anything."

The third man was wonderfully different. He was pleased with the company and proud of its growth. But he was not wholly content. He wanted improvements. All day this third salesman gave me his ideas for getting new business, providing better service to customers, reducing wasted time, revising the compensation plan to give more incentive, all so that he—and the company—would make more. He had mapped out a new advertising campaign he had been thinking about. When I left him, his parting remark was, "I sure appreciate the chance to tell someone about some of my ideas. We've got a good outfit but I believe we can make it better."

My recommendation, of course, was for the third man. It was a recommendation which coincided perfectly with the feelings of the company president. Believe in expansion, efficiency, new products, new processes, better schools, increased prosperity.

Believe in—and push for—progress; and you'll be a leader!

As a youngster, I had an opportunity to see how different thinking of two leaders can make an amazing difference in the performance of followers.

I attended a country elementary school: eight grades, one teacher, and forty children all jammed together inside four brick walls. A new teacher was always a big deal. Led by the *big* boys—the seventh and eighth graders—the pupils set out to see how much they could get away with.

One year there was little more than chaos. Every day there were dozens of the usual school pranks, "wars" of spitballs and paper airplanes. Then there were the major incidents such as locking the teacher outside the school for half a day at the time, or on another occasion the opposite, barricading her within the building for hours. Another day each boy in the upper grades brought his dog into the schoolroom.

Let me add that these children were not delinquents. Stealing, physical violence and deliberate harm were not their objectives. They were healthy kids conditioned by vigorous rural living and needing an outlet for their tremendous pent-up energies and ingenuities.

Well, the teacher somehow managed to stay with the school until the end of that year. To no one's surprise, there was a new teacher the following September.

The new teacher extracted strikingly different performance from the children. She appealed to their personal pride and sense of respect. She encouraged them to develop judgment. Each child was assigned a specific responsibility like washing blackboards or cleaning erasers or practicing on paper-grading for the younger grades. The new teacher found creative ways to use the energy that had been so misdirected a few months before. Her educational program was centered on building character.

Why did the children act like young devils one year and like young angels the next? The difference was the leader, their teacher. In all honesty, we cannot blame the kids for playing pranks an entire school year. In each instance the teacher set the pace.

The first teacher, deep down, didn't care whether the children made progress. She set no goals for the children. She didn't encourage them. She couldn't control her temper. She didn't like teaching so the pupils didn't like learning.

But the second teacher had high, positive standards. She sincerely liked the children and wanted them to accomplish much. She considered each one as an individual. She obtained discipline easily because in everything she did, *she* was well disciplined.

And in each case, the pupils adjusted their conduct to fit the examples set by the teachers.

We find this same form of adjustment taking place every day in adult groups. During World War II military chiefs continually observed that the highest morale was not found in units where commanders were "easy," "relaxed," and "lackadaisical." Crack units were led by officers with high standards who enforced military regulations fairly and properly. Military personnel simply do not respect and admire officers with low standards.

College students, too, take their cue from the examples set by the professors. Students under one professor cut classes, copy term papers, and connive in various ways to pass without serious study. But the same students under another professor willingly work extra hard to master the subject.

In business situations we again find individuals patterning their thinking after that of the superior. Study a group of employees closely. Observe their habits, mannerisms, attitudes toward the company, ethics, self-control. Then compare what you find with the behavior of their superior and you discover amazing similarities.

Every year many corporations that have grown sluggish and are headed downward are rebuilt. And how? By changing a handful of executives at the *top*. Companies (and colleges and churches and clubs and unions and all other types of organizations) are successfully rebuilt from the top down, not from the bottom up. Change the thinking at the top and you automatically change the thinking at the bottom.

Remember this: when you take over leadership of a group, the persons in that group immediately begin to adjust themselves to the standards you set. This is most noticeable during the first few weeks.

Their big concern is to "clue" you in, zero you in, find out what you expect of them. They watch every move you make. They think, how much rope will he give me? How does he want it done? What does it take to please him? How lenient is he? How will he act if I'm late? What will he say if I do this or that?

Once they know, they act accordingly.

Check the example you set. Use this old but ever-accurate quatrain as a guide:

> What kind of world
>   would this world be,
> If everyone in it
>   were just like me?

To add meaning to this self-imposed test, substitute the word *company* for *world* so it reads:

> What kind of company
>   would this company be,
> If everyone in it
>   were just like me?

In similar fashion, ask yourself what kind of club, community, school, church would it be if everyone in it acted like you.

Think, talk, act, live the way you want your subordinates to think, talk, act, live—and they will.

Over a period of time, subordinates tend to become carbon copies of their chief. The simplest way to get high-level performance is to be sure the master-copy is worth duplicating.

Am I a Progressive Thinker?

Check List

A. *Do I think Progressively About My Work?*
   1. Do I appraise my work with the "how can we do it better?" attitude?
   2. Do I praise my company, the people in it, and the products it sells at every possible opportunity?

    3. Are my personal standards with reference to the quantity and quality of my output higher now than 3 or 6 months ago?

    4. Am I setting an excellent example for my subordinates, associates, and others I work with?

B. *Do I think Progressively About My Family?*

    1. Is my family happier today than it was 3 or 6 months ago?

    2. Am I following a plan to improve my family's standard of living?

    3. Does my family have an ample variety of stimulating activities outside the home?

    4. Do I set an example of "a progressive," a supporter of progress, for my children?

C. *Do I think Progressively About Myself?*

    1. Can I honestly say I am a more valuable person today than 3 or 6 months ago?

    2. Am I following an organized self-improvement program to increase my value to others?

    3. Do I have forward-looking goals for at least 5 years in the future?

    4. Am I a booster in every organization or group to which I belong?

D. *Do I think Progressively About My Community?*

    1. Have I done anything in the past six months that I honestly feel has improved my community (neighborhood, churches, schools, etc.)?

    2. Do I boost worthwhile community projects rather than object, criticize, or complain?

    3. Have I ever taken the lead in bringing about some worthwhile improvement in my community?

    4. Do I speak well of my neighbors and fellow citizens?

LEADERSHIP RULE NUMBER 4:
TAKE TIME OUT TO CONFER WITH YOURSELF
AND TAP YOUR SUPREME THINKING POWER.

We usually picture leaders as exceptionally busy people. And they are. Leadership requires being in the thick of things. But while it's usually overlooked, it is noteworthy that leaders spend considerable time alone, alone with nothing but their own thinking apparatus.

Check the lives of the great religious leaders and you'll find each of them spent considerable time alone. Moses frequently was alone, often for long periods of time. So was Jesus. Buddha, Confucius, Mohammed, Gandhi—every outstanding religious leader in history spent much time in solitude away from the distractions of life.

Political leaders, too, those who made history for good or bad, gained insight through solitude. It is an interesting question whether Franklin D. Roosevelt could have developed his unusual leadership capacities had he not spent much time alone while recovering from his polio attack. Harry Truman spent much time as a boy and as an adult alone on a Missouri farm.

Quite possibly Hitler would never have achieved power had he not spent months in jail, alone, where he had time to construct *Mein Kampf,* that brilliantly wicked plan for world conquest that sold the Germans in a blind moment.

Many of the leaders of Communism who have proved to be so diplomatically skillful—Lenin, Stalin, Marx, and many others—spent time in jail where they could, without distraction, plan their future moves.

Leading universities require professors to lecture as few as five hours per week so that they have time to think.

Many outstanding business executives are surrounded all day by assistants, secretaries, telephones, and reports. But follow them around for 168 hours a week and 720 hours a month and you discover they spent a surprising amount of time in uninterrupted thought.

The point is this: the successful person in any field takes time out to confer with himself. Leaders use solitude to put the pieces of a problem together, to work out solutions, to plan, and, in one phrase, to do their super-thinking.

Many people fail to tap their creative leadership power because they confer with everybody and everything else but themselves. You know this kind of person well. He's the fellow who goes to great lengths *not* to be alone. He goes to extremes to surround himself with people. He can't stand being alone in his office, so he goes prowling to see other people. Seldom does he spend evenings alone. He feels a compelling need to talk with others every waking moment. He devours a huge diet of small talk and gossip.

When this person is forced by circumstances to be physically alone, he finds ways to keep from being mentally alone. At times like these he resorts to television, newspapers, radio, telephone, anything that will take over his thinking process for him. In effect he says, "Here, Mr. TV, Mr. Newspaper, occupy my mind for me. I'm afraid to occupy it with my own thoughts."

Mr. I-can't-stand-to-be-alone shuns independent thought. He keeps his own mind blacked out. He is, psychologically, scared of his own thoughts. As time goes by, Mr. I-can't-stand-to-be-alone grows increasingly shallow. He makes many ill-considered moves. He fails to develop firmness of purpose, personal stability. He is, unfortunately, ignorant of the super-power lying unused just behind his forehead.

Don't be a Mr. I-can't-stand-to-be-alone. Successful leaders tap their super-power through being alone. You can, too.

Let's see how.

As part of a professional development program I asked 13 trainees to closet themselves for one hour each day for two weeks. The trainees were asked to shut themselves off from all distractions and think constructively about anything that came to mind.

At the end of two weeks each trainee, without exception, reported the experience proved amazingly practical and worthwhile. One fellow stated that before the managed solitude experiment he was on the verge of a sharp break with another company executive, but through clear thinking he found the source of the problem and the way to correct it. Others reported that they solved problems relating to such varied things as changing jobs, marriage difficulties, buying a home, and selecting a college for a teen-age child.

Each trainee enthusiastically reported that he had gained a much better understanding of himself—his strengths and weaknesses—than he had ever had before.

The trainees also discovered something else that is tremendously significant. *They discovered that decisions and observations made alone in managed solitude have an uncanny way of being 100 per cent right!* The trainees discovered that when the fog is lifted, the right choice becomes crystal clear.

Managed solitude pays off.

One day recently an associate of mine reversed his stand completely on a troublesome issue. I was curious to know why he had switched his thinking, since the problem was very basic. His answer went like this: "Well, I haven't been at all clear in my mind as to what we should do, so I got up at 3:30 this morning, fixed a cup of coffee, and just sat on the sofa and thought until 7:00 A.M. I see the whole matter a lot clearer now. The only thing for me to do is reverse my stand."

His new stand proved completely correct.

Resolve now to set aside some time each day (at least thirty minutes) to be completely by yourself.

Perhaps early in the morning before anyone else is stirring about would be best for you. Or perhaps late in the evening would be a better time. The important thing is to select a time when your mind is fresh and when you can be free from distractions.

You can use this time to do two types of thinking—directed and undirected. To do directed thinking, review the major problem facing you. In solitude your mind will study the problem objectively and lead you to the right answer.

To do undirected thinking, just let your mind select what it wishes to think about. In moments like these your subconscious mind taps your memory bank which in turn feeds your conscious mind. Undirected thinking is very helpful in doing self-evaluation. It helps you get down to the very basic matters like "How can I do better? What should be my next move?"

Remember, the main job of the leader is thinking. And the best preparation for leadership is thinking. Spend some time in managed solitude every day and think yourself to success.

SUMMARY

To Be a More Effective Leader, Put These Four Leadership Principles to Work

1. Trade minds with the people you want to influence. It's easy to get others to do what you want them to do if you'll see things through their eyes. Ask yourself this question before you act: "What would I think of this, if I exchanged places with the other person?"

2. Apply the "Be Human" rule in your dealings with others. Ask, "What is the human way to handle this?" In everything you do, show that you put other people first. Just give other people the kind of treatment you like to receive. You'll be rewarded.

3. Think progress, believe in progress, push for progress. Think improvement in everything you do. Think high standards in everything you do. Over a period of time subordinates tend to become carbon copies of their chief. Be sure the master copy is worth duplicating. Make this a personal resolution: "At home, at work, in community life, if it's progress I'm for it."

4. Take time out to confer with yourself and tap your supreme thinking power. Managed solitude pays off. Use it to release your creative power. Use it to find solutions to personal and business problems. Spend some time alone every day just for thinking. Use the thinking technique all great leaders use. Confer with yourself.

HOW TO USE THE MAGIC OF THINKING BIG IN LIFE'S MOST CRUCIAL SITUATIONS

There is magic in thinking big. But it is so easy to forget. When you hit some rough spots there is danger that your thinking will shrink in size. And when it does, you lose.

Below are some brief guides for staying big when you're tempted to use the small approach.

Perhaps you'll want to put these guides on small cards for even handier reference.

A. *When little people try to drive you down, think big.* To be sure, there are some people who want you to lose, to experience misfortune, to be reprimanded, but these people can't hurt you if you'll remember three things:

1. You win when you refuse to fight petty people. Fighting little people reduces you to their size. Stay big.
2. Expect to be sniped at. It's proof you're growing.
3. Remind yourself that snipers are psychologically sick. Be big. Feel sorry for them.

Think Big Enough to be immune to attacks of petty people.

B. *When that "I-haven't-got-what-it-takes" feeling creeps up on you, think big.* Remember: if you think you are weak, you are. If you think you're inadequate, you are. If you think you're second-class, you are.

Whip that natural tendency to sell yourself short with these tools:

1. Look important. It helps you think important. How you look on the outside has a lot to do with how you feel on the inside.
2. Concentrate on your assets. Build a sell-yourself-on-yourself commercial *and use it*. Learn to supercharge yourself. Know your *positive* self.
3. Put other people in proper perspective. The other person is just another human being, so why be afraid of him?

Think Big Enough to see how good you really are!

C. *When an argument or quarrel seems inevitable, think big.* Successfully resist the temptation to argue and quarrel by:

1. Asking yourself, "Honestly now, is this thing really important enough to argue about?"
2. Reminding yourself, you never gain anything from an argument but you always lose something.

Think Big Enough to see that quarrels, arguments, feuds and fusses will never help you get where you want to go.

D. *When you feel defeated, think big.* It is not possible to achieve large success without hardships and setbacks. But it *is* possible to live the rest of your life without defeat. Big thinkers react to setbacks this way:

1. Regard the setback as a lesson. Learn from it. Research it. Use it to propel you forward. Salvage something from every setback.
2. Blend persistence with experimentation. Back off and start fresh with a new approach.

Think Big Enough to see that defeat is a state of mind, nothing more.

E. *When romance starts to slip, think big.* Negative, petty,

"She's-(He's)-unfair-to-me-so-I'll-get-even" type of thinking slaughters romance, destroys the affection that can be yours. Do this when things aren't going right in the love department.

1. Concentrate on the biggest qualities in the person you want to love you. Put little things where they belong—in second place.
2. Do something special for your mate—and do it often. Think Big Enough to find the secret to marital joys.

   F. When you feel your progress on the job is slowing down, think big. No matter what you do and regardless of your occupation, higher status, higher pay comes from one thing: Increasing the quality and quantity of your output. Do this:

   Think: "I can do better." The best is not unattainable. There is room for doing everything better. Nothing in this world is being done as well as it could be. And when you think, "I can do better," ways to do better will appear. Thinking "I can do better" switches on your creative power.

   Think Big Enough to see that if you put service first, money takes care of itself.

   In the words of Publilius Syrus:

   > A wise man will be Master of His Mind
   > A Fool will be Its Slave

How to Multiply Your Personal Growth Power by Thinking Big*

7

Recently I chatted with a recruitment specialist for one of the nation's largest industrial organizations. Four months each year he visits college campuses to recruit graduating seniors for his company's junior executive training program. The tenor of his remarks indicated he was discouraged about the attitudes of many young men he talked with.

"Most days I interview between 8 and 12 college seniors, all in the upper third of their class, all at least mildly interested in coming with us. One of the main things we want to determine in the screening interview is the individual's self-motivation. We want to find out if he's the kind of fellow who can, in a few years, direct major projects, manage a branch office or plant, or in some other way make a really substantial contribution to the company.

"I must say I'm not too pleased with the personal objectives of most of the young men I talk with. You'd be surprised," he went on, "how many 22-year-olds are more interested in our retirement plan than in anything else we have to offer. A second favorite question is 'Will I move around a lot?' Most of the young men seem to define the word *success* as synonymous with *security*. Can we risk turning our company over to men like that?

---

*David J. Schwartz, *The Magic of Thinking Big* (Englewood Cliffs, N.J.: Prentice-Hall, Inc., 1959).

"The thing I can't understand is why should young people these days be so ultra-conservative, so narrow in their view of the future? Every day there are more signs of expanding opportunity. This country is making record progress in scientific and industrial development. Our population is gaining rapidly. If there ever was a time to be bullish about America, it's now."

The tendency for so many people to think small means there is much less competition than you think for a very rewarding career.

Where success is concerned, people are not measured in inches, or pounds, or college degrees, or family background; they are measured by the size of their thinking. How big we think determines the size of our accomplishments. Now, let's see how we can enlarge our thinking.

Ever ask yourself, "What is my greatest weakness?" Probably the greatest human weakness is self-depreciation—that is, selling oneself short. Self-depreciation shows through in countless ways. John sees a job advertisement in the paper; it's exactly what he would like. But he does nothing about it because he thinks, "I'm not good enough for that job, so why bother." Or Jim wants a date with Joan, but he doesn't call her because he thinks he wouldn't rate with her.

Tom feels Mr. Richards would be a very good prospect for his product, but Tom doesn't call. He feels Mr. Richards is too big to see him. Pete is filling out a job application form. One question asks, "What beginning salary do you expect?" Pete puts down a modest figure because he feels he really isn't worth the bigger sum that he would like to earn.

Philosophers for thousands of years have issued good advice: *Know Thyself*. But most people, it seems interpret this suggestion to mean *Know Only Thy Negative Self*. Most self-evaluation consists of making long mental lists of one's faults, shortcomings, inadequacies.

It's well to know our inabilities, for this shows us areas in which we can improve. But if we know only our negative characteristics we're in a mess. Our value is small.

Here is an exercise to help you measure your true size. I've used it in training programs for executives and sales personnel. It works.

1. Determine your five chief assets. Invite some objective friend to help—possibly your wife, your superior, a professor—some intelligent person who will give you an honest opinion.

(Examples of assets frequently listed are education, experience, technical skills, appearance, well-adjusted home life, attitudes, personality, initiative.)

2. Next under each asset, write the names of three persons you know who have achieved large success but who do *not* have this asset to as great a degree as you.

When you've completed this exercise, you will find you outrank many successful people on at least one asset.

There is only one conclusion you can honestly reach: You're bigger than you think. So, fit your thinking to your true size. Think as big as you really are! Never, never, never sell yourself short!

The person who says "adamantine" when in plain talk he means "immovable" or says "coquette" when we would understand him better if he said "flirt" may have a big vocabulary. But does he have a big thinker's vocabulary? Probably not. People who use difficult, high-sounding words and phrases which most folks have to strain themselves to understand are inclined to be overbearing, and stuffed shirts. And stuffed shirts are usually small thinkers.

The important measure of a person's vocabulary is not the size or the number of words he uses. Rather, the thing that counts, the *only* thing that counts about one's vocabulary, is the effect his words and phrases have on his own and others' thinking.

Here is something very basic: *We do not think in words and phrases. We think only in pictures and/or images.* Words are the raw materials of thought. When spoken or read, that amazing instrument, the mind, automatically converts words and phrases into mind pictures. Each word, each phrase, creates a slightly different mind picture. If someone tells you, "Jim bought a new split-level," you see one picture. But if you're told, "Jim bought a new ranch house," you see still another picture. The mind pictures we see are modified by the kinds of words we use to name things and describe things.

Look at it this way. When you speak or write you are, in a sense, a projector showing movies in the minds of others. And the pictures you create determine how you and others react.

Suppose you tell a group of people, "I'm sorry to report we've failed." What do these people see? They see defeat and all the disappointment and grief the word "failed" conveys. Now suppose you said instead, "Here's a new approach which I think will work." They would feel encouraged, ready to try again.

Suppose you say, "We face a problem." You have created a picture in the minds of others of something difficult, unpleasant to solve. Instead say, "We face a challenge," and you create a mind picture of fun, sport, something pleasant to do.

Or, tell a group, "We incurred a big expense," and people see money spent that will never return. Indeed, this is unpleasant. Instead say, "We made a big investment," and people see a picture of something which will return profits later on, a very pleasant sight.

The point is this: Big thinkers are specialists in creating positive, forward-looking, optimistic pictures in their own minds and in the minds of others. *To think big we must use words and phrases which produce big, positive mental images.*

In the left-hand column below are examples of phrases which create small, negative, depressing thoughts. In the right-hand column the same situation is discussed but in a big, positive way.

As you read these ask yourself: "What mind pictures do I see?"

Phrases Which Create Small, Negative Mind Images	Phrases Which Create Big, Positive Mind Images
1. It's no use, we're whipped.	We're not whipped yet. Let's keep trying. Here's a new angle.
2. I was in that business once and failed. Never again.	I went broke but it was my own fault. I'm going to try again.
3. I've tried but the product won't sell. People don't want it.	So far I've not been able to sell this product. But I know it is good and I'm going to find the formula that will put it over.
4. The market is saturated. Imagine, 75 per cent of the potential has already been sold. Better get out.	Imagine, 25 per cent of the market is still not sold. Count me in. This looks big!
5. Their orders have been small. Cut them off.	Their orders have been small. Let's map out a plan for selling them more of their needs.

Phrases Which Create Small, Negative Mind Images	Phrases Which Create Big, Positive Mind Images
6. Five years is too long a time to spend before I'll get into the top ranks in your company. Count me out.	Five years is not really a long time. Just think, that leaves me 30 years to serve at a high level.
7. Competition has all the advantage. How do you expect me to sell against them?	Competition is strong. There's no denying that, but no one ever has *all* the advantages. Let's put our heads together and figure out a way to beat them at their own game.
8. Nobody will ever want that product.	In its present form, it may not be saleable, but let's consider some modifications.
9. Let's wait until a recession comes along, then buy stocks.	Let's invest now. Bet on prosperity, not depression.
10. I'm too young (old) for the job.	Being young (old) is a distinct advantage.
11. It won't work, let me prove it.	It will work, let me prove it.
The image: Darkness, gloom, disappointment, grief, failure.	The image: Brightness, hope, success, fun, victory.

FOUR WAYS TO DEVELOP THE BIG THINKER'S VOCABULARY

Here are four ways to help you develop a big thinker's vocabulary.

1. Use big, positive, cheerful words and phrases to describe how you feel. When someone asks, "How do you feel today?" and you respond with an "I'm tired (have a headache, wish it were Saturday, don't feel so good)" you actually make yourself feel worse. Practice this: it's a very simple point, but it has tremendous power. Everytime someone asks you, "How are you?" or "How are you feeling today?" respond with a "Just *wonderful!* thanks, and *you?*" or say "Great" or "Fine." Say you feel wonderful at every possible opportunity and you will begin

to feel wonderful—and bigger, too. Become known as a person who always feels great. It wins friends.

2. Use bright, cheerful, favorable words and phrases to describe other people. Make it a rule to have a big, positive word for all your friends and associates. When you and someone else are discussing an absent third party, be sure you compliment him with big words and phrases like "He's really a *fine* fellow." "They tell me he's working out *wonderfully* well." Be extremely careful to avoid the petty cut-him-down language. Sooner or later third parties hear what's been said, and then such talk only cuts *you* down.

3. Use positive language to encourage others. Compliment people personally at every opportunity. Everyone you know craves praise. Have a special good word for your wife or husband everyday. Notice and compliment the people who work with you. Praise, sincerely administered, is a success tool. Use it! Use it again and again and again. Compliment people on their appearance, their work, their achievements, their families.

4. Use positive words to outline plans to others. When people hear something like this: "Here is some *good* news. We face a genuine opportunity . . ." their minds start to sparkle. But when they hear something like "Whether we like it or not, we've got a job to do," the mind movie is dull, boring, and they react accordingly. Promise victory and watch eyes light up. Promise victory and win support. Build castles, don't dig graves!

SEE WHAT CAN BE, NOT JUST WHAT IS

Big thinkers train themselves to see not just what is, but what can be. Here are four examples to illustrate this point.

1. What gives real estate value? A highly successful Realtor who specializes in rural property shows what can be done if we train ourselves to see something where little or nothing presently exists.

"Most of the rural property around here," my friend began, "is run-down and not very attractive. I'm successful because I don't try to sell my prospects a farm as it *is*.

"I develop my entire sales plan around what the farm *can* be. Simply telling the prospect, "The farm has XX acres of bottom land, and XX acres of woods, and is XX miles from town,' doesn't stir him up and make him want to buy it. But when you show him a concrete plan for doing something with the farm, he's just about sold. Here, let me show you what I mean."

He opened his brief case and pulled out a file. "This farm," he said, "is a new listing with us. It's like a lot of them. It's 43 miles from the center of the metropolitan area, the house is run-down, and the place hasn't been farmed in five years. Now here's what I've done. I spent two full days on the place last week just studying it. I walked over the place several times. I looked at neighboring farms. I studied the location of the farm with respect to existing and planned highways. I asked myself, 'What's this farm good for?'

"I came up with three possibilities. Here they are." He showed them to me. Each plan was neatly typed and looked quite comprehensive. One plan suggested converting the farm into a riding stable. The plan showed why the idea was sound: a growing city, more love for the outdoors, more money for recreation, good roads. The plan also showed how the farm could support a sizeable number of horses so that the revenue from the rides would be largely clear. The whole riding stable idea was very thorough, very convincing. The plan was so clear and convincing, I could "see" a dozen couples riding horseback through the trees.

In similar fashion this enterprising salesman developed a second thorough plan for a tree farm and a third plan for a combination tree and poultry farm.

"Now, when I talk with my prospects I won't have to convince them that the farm is a good buy as it is. I help them to see a picture of the farm changed into a money-making proposition.

"Besides selling more farms and selling them faster, my method of selling the property for what it can be pays off in another way. I can sell a farm at a higher price than my competitors. People naturally pay more for acreage *and* an idea than they do for just acreage. Because of this, more people want to list their farms with me and my commission on each sale is larger.

The moral is this: *Look at things not as they are, but as they can be. Visualization adds value to everything. A big thinker always visualizes what can be done in the future. He isn't stuck with the present.*

2. *How much is a customer worth?* A department store executive was addressing a conference of merchandise managers. He was saying,

"I may be a little old-fashioned, but I belong to the school that believes the best way to get customers to come back is to give them friendly, courteous service. One day I was walking through our store when I overheard a sales person arguing with a customer. The customer left in quite a huff.

"Afterwards, the sales person said to another, 'I'm not going to let a $1.98 customer take up all my time and make me take the store apart trying to find her what she wants. She's simply not worth it.'

"I walked away," the executive continued, "but I couldn't get that remark out of my mind. It is pretty serious, I thought, when our sales people think of customers as being in the $1.98 category. I decided right then that this concept must be changed. When I got back to my office, I called our research director and asked him to find out how much the average customer spent in our store last year. The figure he came up with surprised even me. According to our research director's careful calculation, the typical customer spent $362 in our establishment.

"The next thing I did was call a meeting of all supervisory personnel, and explain the incident to them. Then I showed them what a customer is really worth. Once I got these people to see that a customer is not to be valued on a single sale but rather on an annual basis, customer service definitely improved."

The point made by the retailing executive applies to any kind of business. It's repeat business that makes the profit. Often, there's no profit at all on the first several sales. Look at the potential expenditures of the customers, not just what they buy today.

Putting a big value on customers is what converts them into big, regular patrons. Attaching little value to customers sends them elsewhere. A student related this pertinent incident to me, explaining why he'll never again eat in a certain cafeteria.

"For lunch one day," the student began, "I decided to try a new cafeteria that had just opened a couple of weeks before. Nickels and dimes are pretty important to me right now, so I watch what I buy pretty closely. Walking past the meat section I saw some turkey and dressing that looked pretty good, and it was plainly marked 39 cents.

"When I got to the cash register, the checker looked at my tray and said '$1.09.' I politely asked her to check it again because my tally was 99 cents. After giving me a mean glare, she recounted. The difference turned out to be the turkey. She had charged me 49 cents instead of 39 cents. Then I called her attention to the sign which reads 39 cents.

"This really set her off! 'I don't care what that sign says. It's supposed to be 49 cents. See. Here's my price list for today. Somebody back there made a mistake. You'll have to pay the 49 cents.'

"Then I tried to explain to her that the only reason I selected the turkey was because it *was* 39 cents. If it had been marked 49 cents I'd have taken something else.

"To this, her answer was, 'You'll just have to pay the 49 cents.' I did, because I didn't want to stand there and create a scene. But I decided on the spot that I'd never eat there again. I spend about $250 a year for lunches and you can be sure they'll not get one penny of it."

There's an example of the little view. The checker saw one thin dime, not the potential $250.

3. *The case of the blind milkman.* It's surprising how people sometimes are blind to potential. A few years ago a young milkman came to our door to solicit our dairy business. I explained to him that we already had milk delivery service and we were quite satisfied. Then I suggested that he stop next door and talk to the lady there.

To this he replied, "I've already talked to the lady next door, but they use only one quart of milk every two days, and that's not enough to make it worthwhile for me to stop."

"That may be," I said, "but when you talked to our neighbor, did you not observe that the demand for milk in that household will increase considerably in a month or so? There will be a new addition over there that will consume lots of milk."

The young man looked for a moment like he had been struck, and then he said, "How blind can a guy be?"

Today that same one-quart-every-two-days family buys 7 quarts every two days from a milkman who had some foresight. That first youngster, a boy, now has two brothers and one sister. And I'm told there'll be another young one soon.

How blind can we be? See what can be, not just what is.

The school teacher who only thinks of Jimmy as he is—an ill-mannered, backward, uncouth brat—certainly will not aid Jimmy's development. But the teacher who sees Jimmy not as he is now but as he can be will get results.

Most folks driving through Skid Row see only broken-down

stumble-bums hopelessly lost to the bottle. A few devoted people see something else in the Skid Row-ite; they see a reconstructed citizen. And because they see this, they succeed in many cases in doing an excellent rehabilitation job.

4. What determines how much you're worth? After a training session a few weeks ago, a young man came to see me and asked if he could talk with me for a few minutes. I knew that this young fellow, now about 26, had been a very underprivileged child. On top of this, he had experienced a mountain of misfortune in his early adult years. I also knew that he was making a real effort to prepare himself for a solid future.

Over coffee, we quickly worked out his technical problem and our discussion turned to how people who have few physical possessions should look toward the future. His comments provide a straightforward, sound answer.

"I've got less than $200 in the bank. My job as a rate clerk doesn't pay much and it doesn't carry much responsibility. My car is four years old and my wife and I live in a cramped, second-floor apartment.

"But professor," he continued, "I'm determined not to let what I haven't got stop me."

That was an intriguing statement so I urged him to explain.

"It's this way," he went on, 'I've been analyzing people a lot lately and I've noticed this. People who don't have much look at themselves as they are now. That's all they see. They don't see a future, they just see a miserable present.

"My neighbor is a good example. He's continually complaining about having a low-pay job, the plumbing that's always getting fouled up, the lucky breaks somebody else just got, the doctor bills that are piling up. He reminds himself so often that he's poor that now he just assumes that he's always going to be poor. He acts as if he were sentenced to living in that broken-down apartment all the rest of his life."

My friend was really speaking from the heart and after a moment's pause he added, "If I looked at myself strictly as I am—old car, low income, cheap apartment, and hamburger diet—I couldn't help but be discouraged. I'd see a nobody and I'd *be* a nobody for the rest of my life.

"I've made up my mind to look at myself as the person I'm going to be in a few short years. I see myself not as a rate clerk, but as an executive. I don't see a crummy apartment. I see a fine new suburban home. And when I look at myself that way I feel bigger and think bigger. And I've got plenty of personal experiences to prove it's paying off."

Isn't that a splendid plan for adding value to oneself? This young fellow is on the expressway to really fine living. He's mastered this basic success principle: It isn't what one has that's important. Rather, it's how much one is planning to get that counts.

The price tag the world puts on us is just about identical to the one we put on ourselves.

Here is how you can develop your power to see what can be, not just what is. I call these the "practice adding value" exercises.

1. Practice adding value to things. Remember the real estate example. Ask yourself, "What can I do to 'add value' to this room or this house or this business?" Look for ideas to make things worth more. A thing—whether it be a vacant lot, a house, or a business—has value in proportion to the ideas for using it.

2. Practice adding value to people. As you move higher and higher in the world of success, more and more of your job becomes "people development." Ask, "What can I do to 'add value' to my subordinates? What can I do to help them to become more effective?" Remember, to bring out the best in a person, you must first visualize his best.

3. Practice adding value to yourself. Conduct a daily interview with yourself. Ask, "What can I do to make myself more valuable today?" Visualize yourself not as you are but as you can be. Then specific ways for attaining your potential value will suggest themselves. Just try and see.

A retired owner-manager of a medium-sized printing company (60 employees) explained to me how his successor was picked.

"Five years ago," my friend began, "I needed an accountant to head up our accounting and office routine. The fellow I hired was named Harry and was only 26. He knew nothing about the printing business, but his record showed he was a good accountant. Yet a year and a half ago when I retired, we made him President and General Manager of the company.

"Looking back on it, Harry had one trait that put him out in front of everyone else. Harry was sincerely and actively interested in the whole company, not just writing checks and keeping records. Whenever he saw how he could help other employees, he jumped right in.

"The first year Harry was with me, we lost a few men. Harry came to me with a fringe-benefit program which he promised would cut down turnover at low cost. And it worked.

"Harry did many other things, too, which helped the whole company, not just this department. He made a detailed cost study of our production department and showed me how a $30,000 investment in new machinery would pay off. Once we experienced a pretty bad sales slump. Harry went to our sales manager and said, in effect, 'I don't know much about the sales end of the business but let me try to help.' And he did. Harry came up with several good ideas which helped us sell more jobs.

"When a new employee joined us, Harry was right there to help the fellow get comfortable. Harry took a real interest in the entire operation.

"When I retired, Harry was the only logical person to take over.

"But don't misunderstand," my friend continued, "Harry didn't try to put himself over on me. He wasn't a mere meddler. He wasn't aggressive in a negative way. He didn't stab people in the back, and he didn't go around giving orders. He just went around helping. Harry simply acted as if everything in the company affected him. He made company business his business."

We can all learn a lesson from Harry. The 'I'm doing my job and that's enough" attitude is small, negative thinking. Big thinkers see themselves as members of a team effort, as winning or losing with the team, not by themselves. They help in every way they can, even when there is no direct and immediate compensation or other reward. The fellow who shrugs off a problem outside his own department with a comment "Well, that's no concern of mine, let them worry with it," hasn't got the attitude it takes for top leadership.

Practice this. Practice being a big thinker. See the company interest as identical with your own. Probably only a very few persons working in large companies have a sincere, unselfish interest in their company. But after all, only a relatively few persons qualify as big thinkers. And these few are the ones eventually rewarded with the most responsible, best-paying jobs.

Many, many potentially powerful people let petty, small, insignificant things block their way to achievement. Let's look at four examples:

1. What Does It Take to Make a Good Speech?

Just about everyone wishes he had the "ability" to do a first-class job of speaking in public. But most people don't get their wish. Most folks are lousy public speakers.

Why? The reason is simple. Most people concentrate on the small, trivial things of speaking at the expense of the big, important things. In preparing to give a talk, most people give themselves a host of mental instructions like, "I've got to remember to stand straight," "Don't move around and don't use your hands," "Don't let the audience see you use your notes," "Remember, don't make mistakes in grammar, especially don't say 'for he and I', say 'for him and me'," "Be sure your tie is straight," "Speak loudly, but not too loudly," and so on and on.

Now what happens when the speaker gets up to speak? He's scared because he's given himself a terriffic list of things not to do. He gets confused in his talk and finds himself silently asking, "Have I made a mistake?" He is, in brief, a flop. He's a flop because he concentrated on the petty, trivial, relatively unimportant qualities of a good speaker and failed to concentrate on the big things that make a good speaker: *knowledge of what he's going to talk about and an intense desire to tell it to other people.*

The real test of a speaker is not did he stand straight or did he make any mistakes in grammar, but rather did the audience get the points he wanted to put across. Most of our top speakers have petty defects; some of them even have unpleasant voices. Some of the most sought-after speakers in America would flunk a speech course taught by the old negative, "don't do this and don't do that" method.

Yet all these successful public speakers have one thing in common. *They have something to say and they feel a burning desire for other people to hear it.*

Don't let concern with trivia keep you from speaking successfully in public.

2. What Causes Quarrels?

Ever stop to ask yourself just what causes quarrels? At least 99 per cent of the time, quarrels start over petty, unimportant matters like this: John comes home a little tired, a little on edge. Dinner doesn't exactly please him so he turns up his nose and complains. Joan's day wasn't perfect either, so she rallies to her own defense with "Well, what do you expect on my food budget?" or "Maybe I could cook better if I had a new stove like everybody else." This insult's John's pride so he attacks with, "Now, Joan, it's not lack of money; it's simply that you don't know how to manage."

And away they go! Before a truce is finally declared, all sorts of accusations are made by each party. In-laws, sex, money, pre-marital and post-marital promises and other issues will be introduced. Both parties leave the battle nervous, tense. Nothing has been settled and both parties have new ammunition to make the next quarrel more vicious. Little things, petty thinking, cause arguments. So, to eliminate quarrels, eliminate petty thinking.

Here's a technique which works. Before complaining or accusing or reprimanding someone or launching a counterattack in self-defense, ask yourself, "Is it really important?" In most cases, it isn't, and you avoid conflict.

Ask yourself, "Is it really important if he (or she) is messy with cigarettes or forgets to put the top on the toothpaste, or is late coming home?"

"Is it really important if he (she) squandered a little money or invited some people in I don't like?"

When you feel like taking negative action, ask yourself, "Is it really important?" That question works magic in building a finer home situation. It works at the office, too. It works in home-going traffic when another driver cuts in ahead of you. It works in any situation in life that is apt to produce quarrels.

3. John Got the Smallest Office and Fizzled Out

Several years ago, I watched small thinking about an office assignment destroy a young fellow's chances for a profitable career in advertising.

Four young executives, all on the same status level, were moved into new offices. Three of the offices were identical in size and decoration. The fourth was smaller and less elaborate.

J. M. was assigned the fourth office. This turned out to be a real blow to his pride. Immediately he felt discriminated against. Negative thinking, resentment, bitterness, jealousy built up. J. M. began to feel inadequate. The result was that J. M. grew hostile toward his fellow executives. Rather than cooperate he did his best to undermine their efforts. Things got worse. Three months later J. M. slipped so badly, management had no choice but to issue him the pink slip.

Small thinking over a very small matter stopped J. M. In his haste to feel he was discriminated against, J. M. failed to observe that the company was expanding rapidly and office space was at a premium. He didn't stop to consider that the executive who made the office assignments didn't even know which one was the smallest! No one in the organization, except J. M., regarded his office as an index of his value.

Small thinking about unimportant things like seeing your name last on the department route sheet or getting the fourth carbon of an office memo can hurt you. Think big and none of these little things can hold you back.

4. Even Stuttering Is a Detail

A sales executive told me how even stuttering is a mere detail in salesmanship if the fellow has the really important qualities.

"I have a friend, also a sales executive, who loves to play practical jokes, though sometimes these jokes aren't jokes at all. A few months ago a young fellow called on my practical-joking friend and asked for a sales job. The fellow had a terrible stutter though, and my friend deci.'ed right here was a chance to play a joke on me. So the friend told the stammering applicant that he wasn't in the market for a salesman right now but one of his friends (me) had a spot to fill. Then he phoned me and boy, did he give this fellow a build-up. Not suspecting anything, I said, 'Send him right over!'

"Thirty minutes later in he walked. The young fellow hadn't said three words before I knew why my friend was so eager to send him over. 'I-I-I'm J-J-Jack R.,' he said, 'Mr. X sent me over t-t-to talk t-t-to you about a j-j-job.' Almost every word was a struggle. I thought to myself, 'This guy couldn't sell a dollar bill for 90 cents on Wall Street.'

I was sore at my friend but I really felt sorry for this fellow so I thought the least I could do was to ask him some polite questions while I thought up a good excuse as to why I couldn't use him.

"As we talked on, however, I discovered this fellow was no stupe. He was intelligent. He handled himself very nicely, but I just couldn't overlook the fact that he stuttered. Finally, I decided I'd wind up the interview by asking one last question. 'What makes you think you can sell?'

" 'Well,' he said, 'I learn f-f-fast, I-I-I like people, I-I-I think you've got a good company and I-I-I want t-t-to make m-m-money. Now, I-I-I do have a speech im-im-pairment, b-b-but that doesn't b-b-bother me, so why should it b-b-bother anybody else?'

"His answer showed me he had all the really important qualifications for a salesman. I decided right then to give him a chance. And you know, he's working out very well."

Even a speech impairment in a talker's profession is a triviality if the person has the big qualities.

Practice these three procedures to help yourself think above trivialities:

1. Keep your eyes focused on the big objective. Many times we're like the salesman, who, failing to make the sale, reports to his manager, "Yes, but I sure convinced the customer he was wrong." In selling, the big objective is winning sales, not arguments.

In marriage the big objective is peace, happiness, tranquillity— not winning quarrels or saying, "I could have told you so."

In working with employees, the big objective is developing their full potential, not making issues out of their minor errors.

In living with neighbors, the big objective is mutual respect and friendship—not seeing if you can have their dog impounded because once in a while it barks at night.

Paraphrasing some military lingo, it is much better to lose a battle and win the war than to win a battle and lose the war.

Resolve to keep your eyes on the big ball.

2. Ask "Is it really important?" Before becoming negatively excited, just ask yourself, "Is it important enough for me to get all worked up about?" There is no better way to avoid frustration over petty matters than to use this medicine. At least 90 per cent of the quarrels and feuds would never take place if we just faced troublesome situations with "Is this really important?"

3. Don't fall into the triviality trap. In making speeches, solving problems, counseling employees, think of those things that really matter, things that make the difference. Don't become submerged under surface issues. Concentrate on important things.

TAKE THIS TEST TO MEASURE THE SIZE OF YOUR THINKING

In the left column below are listed several common situations. In the middle and right columns are comparisons of how petty thinkers and big thinkers see the same situation. Check yourself. Then decide, which will get me where I want to go? Petty thinking or big thinking?

The same situation handled in two entirely different ways. The choice is yours.

(1) Situation	(2) The Petty Thinker's Approach	(3) The Big Thinker's Approach
Expense Accounts	1. Figures out ways to increase income through chiseling on expense accounts.	1. Figures out ways to increase income by selling more merchandise.
Conversation	2. Talks about the negative qualities of his friends, the economy, his company, the competition.	2. Talks about the positive qualities of his friends, his company, the competition.
Progress	3. Believes in retrenchment or at best the status quo.	3. Believes in expansion.
Future	4. Views the future as limited.	4. Sees the future as very promising.
Work	5. Looks for ways to avoid work.	5. Looks for more ways and things to do, especially helping others.

(1)	(2)	(3)
Situation	The Petty Thinker's Approach	The Big Thinker's Approach
Competition	6. Competes with the best.	6. Competes with the average.
Budget Problems	7. Figures out ways to increase income and buy more of the necessary items.	7. Figures out ways to save money by cutting down on necessary items.
Goals	8. Sets goals high.	8. Sets goals low.
Vision	9. Is preoccupied with the long-run.	9. Sees only the short-run.
Security	10. Regards security as a natural companion of success.	10. Is preoccupied with security problems.
Companionship	11. Surrounds himself with persons with large, progressive ideas.	11. Surrounds himself with petty thinkers.
Mistakes	12. Ignores errors of little consequence.	12. Magnifies minor errors. Turns them into big issues.

IT PAYS IN EVERY WAY TO THINK BIG. REMEMBER!

1. Don't sell yourself short. Conquer the crime of self-deprecation. Concentrate on your assets. You're better than you think you are.

2. Use the big thinker's vocabulary. Use big, bright, cheerful words. Use words that promise victory, hope, happiness, pleasure; avoid words that create unpleasant images of failure, defeat, grief.

3. Stretch your vision. See what people can be, not just what is. Practice adding value to things, to people and to yourself.

4. Get the big view of your job. Think, really think your present job is important. The next promotion depends mostly on how you think about your *present* job.

5. Think above trivial things. Focus your attention on big objectives. Before getting involved in a petty matter, ask yourself "Is it really important?"

GROW BIG BY THINKING BIG!

How to Use the Master Power Play in Every Personal Situation*

8

Let me give you the "Number One Rule" to use in all human relations: *find out what people want and help them get it.* We all have certain basic desires that must be fulfilled to some extent if we are to be completely happy and satisfied. Of these desires, one stands out above all the rest for it is much more than a desire, it is a craving—*the craving to be important.* Psychologists say the desire to be important is the strongest drive in human nature. Mark Twain said it this way: "I have been complimented many times and they always embarrass me; I always feel they have not said enough."

When you find out what a person wants and show him how to get it when he does as you ask, he will follow your orders and carry out your directives every time. That's your primary goal in managing people: to get them to *want* to do what you want them to do. You can do that by helping them fulfill their basic desires.

If you don't know how or where to begin in fulfilling a person's basic desires, here's the place to start. You can always use a person's desire to be important to your advantage. This method will work every time on everyone, with no exceptions. I have yet to meet the person whose actions I cannot influence when I give him that feeling of importance and prestige he needs so much. You can always benefit by helping a person become more important.

---

*James K. Van Fleet, *Van Fleet's Master Guide for Managers* (West Nyack, N.Y.: Parker Publishing Company, Inc., 1978).

WHY A PERSON NEEDS A FEELING OF IMPORTANCE

The desire to be important comes from deep within us. Dr. Sigmund Freud said everything a person does springs from one of two motives: the sex drive and the *desire to be great*. Dr. John Dewey said the deepest urge of all in human nature is the *desire to be important*. Dr Alfred Adler said man wants most of all *to be significant*. William James went even further. He said, "The deepest principle in human nature is the *craving to be appreciated*." Discounting the sex drive since it is primarily a physical need, it is readily apparent that *the greatest motivating force in us all is the desire to be great, the drive to be important*.

I have no degrees in psychology or philosophy, but I agree with the conclusions of these four learned gentlemen. I know from my own practical experience in working with people that everyone wants attention of some kind. Each person wants to be recognized and to be important, no matter who he is. I have never met anyone who did not want to feel important in some way.

Even the person who says he doesn't have any aspirations to be important demands that you listen to his point of view on the subject. He may not want to be important, so he says, but he insists on being heard; he commands your attention. He reminds me of the preacher who said, "You don't have the slightest idea of what the word 'humble' means until you've heard my sermon on humility. I'm the final authority on that subject!"

Every person wants the attention of other people whether he likes to admit that or not. He wants to be listened to; he wants to be heard. He has a deep burning desire—yes, even an insatiable craving—to be important, to be recognized and appreciated. In short, *everybody wants to be somebody*.

You think that's not true in your case? Tell me now, have you ever told a joke, only to have someone butt in and change the subject right when you were in the middle of your story? How did you feel? You'd probably have liked to strangle him, right? Do you really know why you felt that way? Because he was impolite and interrupted you? No. You felt that way because he deflated your ego; he made you feel small, insignificant, and unimportant. He put himself on center stage and shoved you right out of the spotlight.

Let's say you look at a group picture taken at the annual company picnic. Where do your eyes go first? To yourself, of course. Why? Because you are more interested in yourself than in anyone else. That's not criticism, only a simple statement of fact. We all feel the same way about ourselves. From my point of view, I am the center of everything; the world revolves around me. But from your point of view, you are the center of everything; the world revolves around you. And everyone feels the same way you and I do.

If people cannot be important in their jobs or at their work, they will make themselves important elsewhere. They will become lay leaders in church; they will hold offices in lodges and fraternal organizations; some will be active in PTA, Red Cross, and civic affairs.

I will never forget the janitor in a company I once worked for. He had the most menial job in the plant. His clothes were ragged and dirty. No one paid the slightest bit of attention to him. But when he left the plant at the end of the day, what a metamorphosis. He wore the latest, most fashionable slacks and sports jacket. He was bathed, shaved, and well-groomed. And he drove off in a flashy red foreign sports car!

You would do well, then, to keep the following thoughts in mind when dealing with people.

1. Every person is an egotist. He demands attention, appreciation, and recognition of some sort.

2. Each individual is more interested in himself than in anyone else.

3. Each person's viewpoint is that he is the center of everything. The world revolves around him.

4. Everyone you meet wants to feel important and amount to something.

5. Each man has to be needed in some way by others. He wants to feel indispensable in his job, home, church, or club. He likes to feel others just couldn't get along without him.

6. We all need respect and approval from others before we can have respect for and approval of ourselves.

7. Each person will do everything necessary to gain the attention and recognition he needs so much so that he can feel more important.

When you sincerely feed a person's ego and fulfill his desire to be important, you'll achieve these worthwhile benefits:

1. Each person will go all out to help you attain your goals.
2. You'll gain many, many true friends.
3. You'll have no enemies.
4. People will admire you and respect you.
5. Your people will always do what you ask them to do; they'll give you their full support.
6. You'll win your people's hearts as well as their heads.
7. You'll find this master power play works like magic; it literally performs miracles with people.

TECHNIQUES YOU CAN USE TO GAIN THESE BENEFITS

An Old-Fashioned Technique that Will Never Go out of Style

Do you want a person to give you his unswerving loyalty and full support? Do you expect to receive his complete cooperation and willing obedience? Would you like him to have confidence in you and respect you? Then all you need do is *praise him*, not just once, but all the time, over and over again.

Praise him. Tell him what a magnificent job he's doing for you . . . how much you need him . . . how you can't get along without him . . . how happy you are he's with your organization.

We all hunger for a word of praise. We all need recognition and appreciation. Everybody likes a compliment. No one is immune. As Mark Twain once said, "I could live for two months on one good compliment."

Be generous with your praise. Pass it around freely; the supply is limited only by you. Don't be stingy about passing out bouquets; they cost you nothing. Above all, never act as if you expected something in return for your praise. Don't pay a person a compliment as if you wanted a receipt for it.

Praise is the best way to make a person feel important. Criticism is the quickest way to destroy a person and make him your enemy. If you criticize a person, he will soon hate you. Nothing is more destructive to a person's pride than criticism. Listen to Carla Evans, a store manager for Fairfield Fashions in St. Louis, Missouri, as she tells why she uses praise instead of criticism with her employees.

> "Some people say they find it hard to praise a person, but I disagree with that," Carla says. "It's actually quite easy to find something to compliment in a person and make her feel more important. All you need do is look for something good about the individual.
>
> "For instance, you can say, 'You really handled that difficult customer skillfully, Jane . . . That's really a top-notch idea, Fran . . . I sure appreciate your getting that report out ahead of time, Alice . . . Thanks for staying late and getting those letters out yesterday, Mary . . .'
>
> "See how easy it is? It all depends on what you're looking for. If you want to praise a person and make her feel important, you can always find something to compliment her for. If you want to criticize her, you can always find something wrong, too. But I'd rather praise than criticize. I find it's a much better way to get my employees to do their best for me."

I agree with Carla. I never criticize anyone, either. I have enough character defects of my own to worry about without taking someone else's inventory. I do make helpful suggestions or show a person how to improve his work methods, but I do not use criticism to do that. I always go out of my way to praise a person, but I am extremely reluctant to find fault.

It would be wise to remember that no person ever criticizes himself for anything, no matter how wrong he might be. He will always find some excuse to justify his actions. If a person will not accept criticism even from himself, then I know he will never accept it from me. However, I do not want to mislead you here. Let me quickly point out that my hesitancy to criticize others will not stop me from taking the necessary corrective or disciplinary action when it's required.

FIVE SMALL WORDS YOU CAN USE
TO MAKE A PERSON FEEL IMPORTANT

I Am Proud Of You are five of the most valuable and powerful words in the English language. You can use them any time on your employees, associates, and friends, or your husband, wife, and children. Just tell them how proud you are of something they did. Be generous with your compliments. They cost you nothing . . . they'll pay you rich dividends.

These five little words will work miracles in human relations for you. You can even use them with your boss. If you feel too self-conscious to say "I'm proud of you" to him, change the words and say, "I'm sure proud to work for you." They'll still produce the same good results you're after.

Does this method work? I'll say it does. I'm not the only one to use it either. George Wheeler, executive vice-president and general manager of a radio and television factory in Missouri, uses it, too.

> "I've never found any better words to use with my employees than 'I'm proud of you,' " George says. "That's one of the highest compliments you can pay a person.
>
> "When an employee does an exceptionally fine piece of work or turns in a terriffic money-saving or cost-cutting idea, just to say 'Thanks' isn't enough. I go to him right out on the production line and in front of all his fellow workers I pat him on the back and say, 'Thanks a lot for what you did, Bill; *I'm really proud of you.*' He'll work even harder for me from then on. So will everyone else. They want some of that sweet syrup, too."

A Psychological Study Proves the Value of This Priceless Technique

I want to show you exactly why praise is such a valuable procedure to make a person feel important. I'll also show you why criticism is such a useless method. A team of psychologists from the University of Missouri made a detailed study to determine the relative merits of these two techniques. Here's how they conducted their study and the conclusions they reached.

The team of psychologists carried out their tests with army recruits in the reception station at Fort Leonard Wood, Missouri, a basic training center for the United States Army. Three thousand young men, still fresh from all walks in civilian life, were tested in their first 48 hours at the reception center before they were sent down to their training units to be indoctrinated by tough army drill sergeants with army customs and procedures. The team tested 60 men a day for 10 weeks. Here's how they ran their tests.

Each morning 60 volunteers were divided into six squads of 10 men each. The squads were then given the same set of difficult tasks to perform. As each one completed its work, it was judged on its performance. But the results of each squad were reviewed in different ways by the testing team.

Squad number 1 was praised in public before all the rest of the squads. The second squad was also praised, but in private with only its own members present. Squad number 3 was criticized in private; only its own members were present. Number 4 was publicly criticized in front of all the other squads. The fifth squad was ridiculed and made fun of in private with only its own squad there. Squad number 6 was ridiculed and made fun of in front of all 60 volunteers.

The squads were then given the same exact work to do again. Their second performance was checked against the first. The second performance results are shown as follows:

Squad #	Critique Method	% Showing Improvement on Second Test
1	Public Praise	90%
2	Private Praise	75%
3	Private Criticism	49%
4	Public Criticism	31%
5	Private Ridicule	19%
6	Public Ridicule	10%

The results are quite clear. Praise is a much better tool to use than either criticism or ridicule when you're trying to motivate a person to upgrade his performance. When you praise people in public, nine out of ten will improve, for you've given them the recognition they need so much. You've made them feel more important in front of other people. Praise in private will not do quite as well as public praise, but three out of four will still respond favorably.

However, if you criticize people hoping to get improvement, you will always fail. Even when you criticize in private, only about half the people will improve and do a better job for you. If you criticize people publicly in front of others, less than one-third will show any sign of doing better. No one wants to be disapproved of or have his faults criticized, including me.

If one of your people asks you to look at his work and let him know where he's making his mistakes, don't be misled. That isn't what he wants at all. He wants you to tell him how well he's doing. He wants you to pat him on the back and tell him he's not making any mistakes. He wants to be praised, not criticized. Read between the lines; listen to what he really said. Remember those basic desires every person has. *To be criticized is not one of them.*

Criticism causes the criticized person to do worse; it destroys his incentive to improve. Most people can't criticize without hurting the other person's feelings. They usually do more harm than good. As Josh Billings, the American humorist, said, "To be a critic demands more brains than most people have." You can't criticize another person without deflating his ego and destroying his feeling of importance. Criticism maims and cripples people psychologically. *The best thing to remember about criticism is to forget it.*

Ridicule, either public or private, is a complete waste of time as you can see from the last two figures on the chart. However, I want to take some time here to tell you exactly why ridicule is so useless. You'll be better able to understand one basic desire when I do.

You see, a man will tolerate almost any insult, defeat, or injury, and accept it with some semblance of good grace. You can steal his wife, his job, his money, and although he won't like you for it, he'll probably tolerate it up to a point and still treat you like a civilized human being.

But if you make fun of a man, if you belittle and ridicule him, or if you make a fool of him—especially in front of others—you'll have made an enemy for the rest of your life. He'll never forget and he'll never forgive, for you've absolutely devastated his sense of self-respect, dignity, and self-esteem as well as deflated his ego and injured his pride. Besides these two, you've also destroyed his opportunity to fulfill no less than four more of his basic desires. You've taken away the possibility of being recognized for his efforts by ridiculing him instead of praising him . . . you've destroyed him in front of his peers and prevented the group from approving of him . . . you've ruined his desire to accomplish something worth while . . . you've taken away his feeling of emotional security. Can you blame him now for despising you? Look at the amount of harm you've done to him just by ridiculing and making fun of him.

If you do ridicule someone and make fun of him, better load your shotgun, bolt the doors, and place a guard at every window. He'll come after you for sure. The basic desire for revenge, vengeance, an eye for an eye and a tooth for a tooth, can be a greater driving force than even the desire for importance or the desire for sex.

Why This Powerful Praise Technique Works So Well

This study by the University of Missouri psychologists confirms something I have known and practiced for many years. *Public praise is the most powerful technique you can use to feed a person's ego and make him feel more important.* Let's dig a little deeper into this technique and find out exactly why praise works so well.

Praise Releases Energy; Praise Acts as an Energizer. That's exactly why it works so well. To praise means to honor, compliment, pay recognition to, express approval of. If you are praised, what is your reaction? Probably the same as mine. You feel thrilled and excited. You're happy you were able to please someone. Praise increases your enthusiasm; it makes you want to do even better. You work harder than before so you can get more of it. So will your people.

Do you see how praise releases energy? Praise makes a person work harder, more efficiently, and with greater enthusiasm. That was proven some time ago by Dr. Henry H. Goddard, an American psychologist.

Dr. Goddard performed his experiments when he was research director at New Jersey's Vineland Training School for Retarded Children. Dr. Goddard used an ergograph to measure energy and fatigue. When tired children were praised and complimented for their work, the ergograph showed an immediate upward surge of new energy. But when they were criticized and reprimanded, the ergograph readings were immediately lowered.

You don't need an ergograph to measure the release of new energy in your employees. Just praise them; you can see the good results. For instance, when you praise your secretary for her typing skills and abilities, you'll find fewer errors than ever in your correspondence. Those letters will also be ready for your signature much sooner than before. Tell your subordinates what good jobs they've done, praise them in front of their fellows, and they'll do even better work for you next time. This technique will work with your wife, husband, children, relatives, friends, anyone. The final proven conclusion is that *praise releases new energy in a person.*

OTHER BASIC DESIRES THAT ARE AUTOMATICALLY FULFILLED BY THIS TECHNIQUE

Not only does praise feed a person's ego and fulfill his desire to be important, but it also satisfies other basic desires.

1. Recognition of efforts, reassurance of worth.
2. Social or group approval; acceptance by one's peers.
3. A sense of roots, belonging somewhere.
4. The accomplishment of something worth while.
5. A sense of self-esteem, dignity, and self-respect.
6. The desire to win, to be first, to excel.
7. Emotional security.

You can see from this why praise is one of the most powerful techniques you can ever use to get a person to do what you want him to do. You just can't miss when you praise someone for what he's done.

Praising Every Single Improvement

Smart animal trainers know you must praise every single improvement with a kind word of encouragement, a pat on the head, and a bit of food if further progress is to be made. If we know enough to praise animals for every single improvement they make, we ought to be wise enough to use the same technique on people.

Get in the habit of praising even the slightest improvement in your employees. That will inspire them to keep right on improving. Don't wait until someone does something really outstanding or unusual before you praise him. Praise the tiniest bit of progress you can find.

I've been married to my wife for more than 35 years now and she's a wonderful cook. But it wasn't always that way. The first month or so was, well . . . anyway, I haven't had a bad meal since then. Do you know why? Because to this very day I never get up from the table without saying, "Thanks a lot, honey; that was really a terrific meal." That's why I always eat too well.

The words "Thank you" can work magic in human relations when you use them properly. They will always make people glad they did something for you, especially when you use them sincerely. You can soup them up a bit by saying "Thanks very much . . . thanks a million . . . thanks a lot . . . I sure do appreciate it." Look the person right in the eye when you're thanking him. If he's worth being thanked, he's worth being looked at and noticed. Don't be like the checkout clerk in the supermarket who says thank you to the cash register and never sees the customer.

Keep your eyes open and find things to thank people for. Every time you say "Thank you," you're praising the other person. You're giving him credit for having done something you appreciate. When you let people know how grateful you are for what they've done, when you praise every single improvement they make, no matter how small, they will want to do even more for you.

Praise the slightest improvement a person makes and praise every improvement he makes. As Charles Schwab would say, "I am anxious to praise but loath to find fault. If I like anything, I am always hearty in my approbation and lavish in my praise."

Using Sincere Praise Instead of Flattery

To flatter a person means to praise him beyond what is true or to praise him insincerely. The dictionary says flattery is praise that is usually untrue or overstated. In other words, to flatter is simply to lie. To be sincere means to be genuine and honest, free from pretense or deceit.

Flattery is as phony as a three-dollar bill. It's counterfeit and worthless. It avails you nothing. People will spot your phoniness and see through you immediately. You would be far better off to praise a person for some small thing and be sincere about it than to pick out something big and lie about it.

Why do people use flattery when it's so worthless? Usually because the individual who flatters another is too lazy to look for something good and worthwhile the other individual has done.

There's a quick and easy way to know whether you're praising a person or flattering him. Flattery praises a person for what he *is*, not what he does. When you use sincere praise, you do just the opposite. You praise a person for what he *does*, not what he is. Look at the following examples. You'll see exactly what I mean.

FLATTERY: Tom, you're the best salesman in the whole outfit.

PRAISE: Congratulations, Tom. You had the most sales in the entire district last month. That's an outstanding record. Thanks a lot for your excellent work. I sure do appreciate it.

FLATTERY: Miss Jones, you are really the most beautiful typist in the whole world.

PRAISE: Miss Jones, your typing is absolutely superb. I have no hesitancy at all about signing my correspondence now. I really do appreciate your excellent work. Thanks a lot.

FLATTERY: George, you're the smartest worker in the whole plant.

PRAISE: George, that suggestion of yours was a brilliant idea. It's going to save us a lot of unnecessary steps. Thanks a million for your help.

See the difference here? Flattery is vague, ill-defined, indefinite, and usually confusing. It leaves the flattered person wondering *Why? How? In What Way?* He doesn't know what he's actually done to deserve the praise, so he's in no position to repeat his performance. Flattery does nothing at all to help the person improve his work methods. It's really the lazy man's way of doing things, for nothing at all is said about what the person does, only about what he *is*. That requires no effort at all; anyone can do that.

When you praise a person for what he *does*, not for what he is, you are forced to find something to praise him for. Genuine praise requires thought, energy, and effort on your part, but it's well worth it in the long run.

Praising a person for what he does helps in many other ways, too.

First, the individual being praised knows exactly what he's being praised for. Second, when you praise a person for a certain act, you are forced to be sincere. Third, praising the act instead of the person helps you avoid charges of favoritism or prejudice.

Praising a person for what he does also saves him embarrassment. People tend to feel awkward and ill at ease if you say they're the greatest of all or they're better than anyone else. When you pick out something specific he's done and congratulate him for it, he feels good about it. There's nothing for him to be embarrassed about.

Some managers don't use praise often enough. They say praise makes people egotistical, conceited, and swell-headed. They think too much praise makes it ordinary and commonplace like turning diamonds into sand. Then they bend too far the other way and become too stingy with their compliments. I can say without hesitation that managers who feel this way have never learned to praise a person properly. They are using flattery—not sincere praise.

Remember to praise a person for what he *does*, not what he is. Praise him for his good work; he'll do his job even better and faster for you than before. As long as you praise the act and not the person, you'll have no trouble. That's the big difference between sincere praise and phony flattery.

HOW YOU CAN USE PRAISE TO CORRECT MISTAKES

I'll have more to say about constructive criticism later on. Here I want to show you how to use praise to correct a person's mistakes gracefully so there'll be no hard feelings whatever.

The key to this is to *praise a person at the same time you're pointing out his error.* Here are some examples of both the right and the wrong way to correct a person's mistakes.

RIGHT: Miss Jones, your typing is outstanding. You make very few errors and your work is clean and neat. Your spelling is exceptionally accurate. However, I did find one small mistake in this letter. It's not a big one, but unfortunately, it does change the exact meaning of what I wanted to say. . . .

WRONG: Miss Jones, you are without a doubt the worst typist I've
             ever had in this office. I'm sick and tired of your stupid
             mistakes. Now do this letter over and get it right this time!

RIGHT: Joe, you did outstanding work on this difficult project on
             such short notice. I know you were under a lot of pres-
             sure, but I've found one thing here I don't seem to under-
             stand. I wonder if you'd mind checking this measurement
             again for accuracy. It seems to me to be a little off. If it is,
             I'm afraid the whole thing could be thrown out of whack.

WRONG: What the hell is wrong with you, Joe? These measure-
             ments of yours are all screwed up again. Of all the idiotic,
             stupid people I have to work with, I swear you're the
             worst. Now do it over and get it right this time or else!

RIGHT: Tim, your report card really looks terrific this time. I'm
             really proud of your work. Your history grade is the only
             one that's off a little, but I know you can bring that up,
             too, when I see how well you've done in your other sub-
             jects.

WRONG: Why do you get such stupid low grades in history,
             dummy? You're either too lazy or too stupid to learn.
             Which one is it? What's wrong with you? You'd better
             shape up quick!

Whenever you correct the person instead of the act, you get
angry. You automatically use sarcasm and ridicule. Words like *stupid*,
lazy, *dumb*, and *idiot* creep into the conversation. Remember when
the team of psychologists from the University of Missouri used ridicule
on the trainees at Fort Leonard Wood, improvement fell to as low as
10 percent on the second performance.

If you think the language of these wrong statements in the examples I've given you is too strong, let me tell you I've heard much worse
four-letter words used by managers and supervisors, even by top-level
executives. I've heard every cuss word or obscenity that's ever been
invented by man to criticize and castigate another human being. I've
heard everything from "Damn you" to words questioning a man's

legitimacy at birth and some derogatory terms about his mother's status.

So always correct a person's mistakes by using praise. That way, you don't destroy a person's dignity and self-respect. You've let him save face. It takes time, patience, and understanding to use this method, but the end results are well worth the efforts expended.

As you can plainly see, I'm definitely high on praise, for I've found it to be an absolutely outstanding technique to use to make a person feel more important. I know from experience it works wonders with people. However, you can use a few other techniques to make a person feel important. I'd like to discuss several of them with you right now.

ASKING A PERSON FOR HIS OPINION, HIS ADVICE, AND HIS HELP

One of the quickest ways to make a person feel more important is simply to ask him for his help or his advice. All you need say is "What's your opinion on this?" You'll send even the janitor home bragging to his wife that the company president had to come to him for help in solving a problem.

A note of caution here. When you do ask for someone's opinion, listen courteously to what he says. I don't care how outlandish his idea sounds to you, listen to him carefully. Hear him out to the end. Don't disagree with him as soon as he's finished. Even though you might know his idea won't work, don't tell him so. You'll injure his pride, deflate his ego, and spoil everything if you do.

When he's finished, thank him sincerely for his help and advice. Tell him you'll give every possible consideration to his idea. You'll find when you do listen to your employee's opinions, they'll go all out to think up new and better ways of doing things. This can be extremely profitable and beneficial for you. Listening to people for new ideas is a lot like panning gold. You see a lot more sand than gold, but when you do find a nugget, it can really be exciting.

Frankly speaking, I do not like a suggestion box. Nor does Paul King, Director of Research and Development for Suncoast Solar Energy Technologies, in Miami, Florida.

"I know most companies use suggestion boxes to get new ideas from employees," Paul says. "We used to have one, but we got rid of it. It was just too impersonal. Besides, a person never knew whether his suggestion was actually read or thrown away in the trash at the end of the day.

"I keep my office door open all the time. Any employee can come in whenever he feels he has a worthwhile idea to contribute. If it's complicated requiring a lot of sketches or narrative description, he gets every bit of assistance he needs from our office staff. When we first started this program, we got a lot of ideas we couldn't utilize, but our people soon settled down. Now when someone comes in my office, chances are good he has something we can really use."

I've seen Paul's office and when he says he keeps an open door at all times, he really means it. The door has been completely removed and taken away! John De Butts, chairman of the board for AT&T, keeps an open door, too. He says it has been a major factor in his successful business career.

Keeping an open door is an excellent way to make people feel important. Such a policy lets your employees know you're really interested in them and in what they have to offer you. They feel they have access to you, that they can bring you their ideas and their problems, and that you'll listen to them. An open door says a lot to your employees about the kind of person you are.

MAKING A PERSONNEL PROBLEM A "PERSONAL" PROBLEM

A sign on Al Miller's desk reads: MAKE PERSONNEL ACTIONS PERSONAL TRANSACTIONS. Al is personnel manager for a firm in Birmingham, Alabama. He believes sincerely you cannot be a good personnel worker if you don't have a deep compassion for people and their personal problems.

"Everyone wants to be treated as an important person," Al says. "No one wants to be just another number—some nameless anonymity. Every person wants to retain his own individual identity. Unfortunately, in today's automated and mechanized world, a person often becomes just like another piece of office equipment or an extension of some part of the machinery. Here at Hamilton Industries, we do everything we can to keep that from happening. We want to treat every employee as a very important person—a real VIP. We follow a set of specific guidelines to insure that every personnel action is a personal transaction."

Al was good enough to let me use those guidelines. I'm sure you will find them useful. I know that I did.

How to Make Every Personnel Action a "Personal" Transaction

Special Instructions: Before you complete any personnel action, answer the following questions, sign your name, and attach this questionnaire as a cover sheet to the individual's personnel action file.

1. Have you treated the other person as you'd like to be treated if the situation were reversed?
2. Did you handle this piece of paper with a name on it as a person—or just another piece of paper?
3. Did you really answer all the individual's questions, or did you leave him in doubt about some of your answers?
4. When you weren't sure, did you get help from someone else? Whose assistance did you ask for?
5. Did you weigh each case on its own individual merits without bias or prejudice?
6. When you gave your answer, were you justly proud of the understanding and tolerance you showed in your decision?
7. If you couldn't go along with the person's request, did you tell him why?
8. Did you do everything you could do to help the person solve his problem?
9. Are you truly proud of what you said to the person and how you said it?

10. Can you sign your name willingly to this personnel action without any reservation or hesitation of any sort?

Making the Other Person a Real VIP

As Al Miller said, it's hard in today's automated and mechanized world to keep from being regarded as another piece of office equipment or an extension of some part of the machinery. Even off the job, a person tends to become a nonentity more than ever before since computers depend on numbers rather than names for credit, identification, and billing purposes. Today, people just don't seem to be as important as individuals as they used to be, and that makes them hungrier than ever for attention and a feeling of importance.

You might be San Sloditski or Susie Carmichael to some people, but to the electric company you're account number 334-40-89085. Trying to win an argument with a computer over how much you owe on your revolving charge account can be one of the most frustrating and nerve-wracking situations you'll ever get into. It can really make you feel small and insignificant when you have to stoop to the point of doing battle with a machine. Of course, the final insult comes when you lose the fight.

A person will go to great extremes to be heard and noticed and gain attention from others simply from the fear of being ignored and not listened to. The social bore who talks only about himself and his own achievements and the neighborhood bully down the street both suffer from this same fear although the outward symptoms seem so much different on the surface.

The desire to be important and the fear of not succeeding at it are such driving forces in everyone you can readily use that fact to your own advantage. Make every one of your employees a very important person and he'll do whatever you ask him to do. You can make each individual in your organization a VIP when you use the following techniques:

1. Give your whole-hearted attention to the other person. Rejection hurts; attention heals. It's just that simple.
2. Encourage him to talk about himself and his own interests. That shows him how important he is to you.

3. Give each individual the special identity he desires by letting him know he's both wanted and needed by you.

4. Remember a person's name. Never degrade it or make fun of it with ethnic jokes; it's his most important and valuable possession.

5. Never take another person for granted. It's one of the quickest ways to reject a person and make him your enemy.

6. Get your mind off yourself and what you want. You'll get what you want when you give him what he wants—your attention.

How to Chart
and Cash in on Your   9
Personal Success Cycle*

Oddly enough, even the seemingly elusive quality of success has an ebb-and-flow rhythm. Just as "The Music Goes 'Round and 'Round"—or the rotor on an electric light meter twirls when in use, so does the transient wand of success touch each and every one of us at varying intervals of time.

When Lincoln first ventured into his professional career he declared, "I will prepare and some day my chance will come." Shakespeare phrased the same idea in the soliloquy of Brutus in *Julius Caesar*:

> *There is a tide in the affairs of men,*
> *Which, taken at the flood, leads on to fortune;*
> *Omitted, all the voyage of their life*
> *Is bound in shallows and in miseries.*

Therefore, one of the first requisites in learning to think like a millionaire is to make a firm and very determined resolution to be an outstanding expert in *something*—but whatever old or new and untried activity you center upon, resolve with great will to learn and assimilate all there is to know about the subject you have chosen.

---

*Howard E. Hill, *How to Think like a Millionaire and Get Rich* (West Nyack, N.Y.: Parker Publishing Company, Inc., 1968).

This single, intensely directed interest in any given field of endeavor has never yet failed to produce a boundless richness of mind as well as enormous holdings of wealth plus an achievement record well-noted by one's contemporaries.

HOW TO USE SELECTIVE CURIOSITY

Two words that adequately describe the millionaire potential are *selective curiosity*.

It is important to differentiate between the ordinary trait of nosiness and the powerful highly-energized characteristic of a strongly-motivated quest for knowledge within a specialized area of endeavor. This tendency to probe, to study and compare, to research, and to inquire into every phase of given activity, is the one essential quality that separates the men from the dreamers in the quest for success, achievement, and great wealth.

This urge to know, as expressed in the careers of successful men and women, embraces every imaginable field of activity including salesmanship, business, the trades, and even the professions that demand a long and tedious period of preparation. I like to tell the story of a janitor in a great Eastern school of medicine who once nurtured an insatiable thirst for learning all there was to know about healing the sick. In seeking his ultimate fulfillment, this man began to collect from every classroom in the building assigned to him for clearing textbooks that had been discarded by the students. At night, in his lonely basement room in the dormitory this chap would read and study endlessly—until one day he was publicly recognized by this same university as one of the outstanding diagnosticians of his time—even though he did not hold a formal degree in medicine.

In another instance, I once knew a young fellow who had a burning desire to own his own print shop. To begin with, this man knew nothing about the trade, but he did possess one priceless ingredient of character—selective curiosity. Out of his meagre earnings as a day laborer on the shipping docks of a trucking company, he began to read everything he could get his hands on pertaining to the trade. By literally saving his pennies he was one day able to acquire a small handpress, a few sticks of furniture to help compress and hold type within a given space, and one font of old type. With an apparently dismal start, this man began to attract other items associated with the craft until one day he was able to take the big plunge and open a modest little shop of his own. Today this determined individual is the full owner of a large and flourishing printing business.

There are innumerable "little success stories" just like these to be found in nearly every walk of life. *The same can be done by you*—but you are the only person in the world who can set this success cycle with its magic wand moving toward you and your enterprises.

MAKE THESE FIVE MOVES AND YOU ARE "ON THE BANDWAGON"

1. Resolve to increase your wealth potential each and every day even if all you do is add one penny to your capital account. When you perform this act of adding to, know that it is for the purpose of establishing a pattern of daily growth.

2. Resolve to raise your level of money consciousness to the height of one million dollars—and learn to keep your attitudes oriented to this high plateau of achievement.

3. Direct your attention to the broad field of human interests and determine precisely what it is that you are going to grow with—be it animal, flower, food, flowers, a service, a trade, a profession, or a device. Regardless of what it is, what you choose is to be your one-way ticket to whatever it is that you want to accomplish.

4. Decide to follow the growth patterns as described in each of the steps to thinking like a millionaire, in the exact order as they are given herein.

5. Develop your own time plan of growth. In brief, this means to set forth in your own blueprint for personal progress the list of accomplishments that you must acquire in order to reach your goal—with the full understanding that a great success is founded upon the law of minor achievement. In practice this means that the summit of complete fulfillment can only be attained by adding together hundreds of little successes.

Once you are on the bandwagon of increase there can be no limit to how far you can go. You set the goal and the wagon begins to move irresistibly.

One Man Started With a Handful of Montana Wheat

Back at the turn of the century, Thomas Donald Campbell, a small cattle rancher, regarded a handful of scrawny plains wheat. What he saw did not please him, so he determined to do something about it. He set himself the task of applying modern methods of agriculture to the growing of better wheat, with a greater yield per acre. Before too long he was confronted with the necessity of applying the newly invented techniques of mechanization to his farm operations. The lists of his attainments are legion, and the results of his keen interest in a few grains of wheat have made history.

When Campbell passed away recently he was farming 95,000 acres of land in Montana and directing the operation of a land holding in New Mexico that totaled close to a half-million acres. For these achievements he was widely regarded as "America's Wheat King." All because he directed a strong selective curiosity toward the prime ingredient of a loaf of bread—a human need that has prevailed since the beginning of time.

In between there were endless minor achievements, but the pinnacle of his growth was attained when more than a dozen foreign governments recognized his genius, including such nations as Russia, Britain, and France, and engaged him to assist in the development of millions of acres of farm land in which the principles of soil management, crop rotation, and mechanization were put into practice.

HOW TO GET INTO THE SUCCESS CYCLE

Probably the first thought that occurs to you will be: "This is going to take some doing." In truth, however, the ticket that is needed to get into the full rhythm of success is so close, and so obvious, that all too many persons look right past a dozen opportunities to grow rich each and every day. Again, all that you need to do is direct your undivided attention toward any item that sparks your interest and then apply the three-point system of evaluation explained in the next few paragraphs.

Getting the right answer might demand a bit of study, but the rewards are so immense that the trifle of effort required is of little consequence.

The Three-Point System of Evaluation

1. Is the item you have selected practical? In other words, is it even with or just a little ahead of present trends in human interest? To select an idea, a product, service, or a device that is too far in advance of acceptance is to load yourself down with an impossible burden of sales and distribution problems and you will further handicap yourself because of the need for heavy advertising expenditures. Make certain that what you have in mind is almost ready to ride the crest of popular demand. How to do this most effectively is fully explained in the Fifth Step.

2. Is the item you have selected in or near a basic human want? Perhaps the buying public doesn't know that it wants, much less needs, your product or idea, but testing can often reveal the answer. Employ all of the techniques explained in Step Five when you are far enough along to make this part of your working equipment.

3. What is the growth or profit potential of the product, device, service, or idea that sparks your interest? And there is still another question that should back up this first query: Is this idea of yours likely to hit now, or will it take years of hard work?

The essential challenge is this: "Is what I have in mind better, bigger, faster, lovelier? Does it provide a chance for greater returns, or insure an easier way of life?"

Why is this careful review necessary? For example, in the food and grocery business alone last year more than 2500 new products were introduced to the buying public, and out of this number more than a thousand items were discarded for the very plain reason that the housewife didn't cotton to the idea. Unfortunately, most of these discards came from firms or persons who dived headlong into the production of a product simply because it appealed to them. In other words then, when you are truly thinking like a millionaire you will first learn to evaluate correctly.

You might be justified in claiming that anything you choose will get you into the full rhythm of the success cycle, but let's take a closer look.

Grab a Brass Ring

When I first proclaimed the theory of "anything goes" in a talk to the Beverly Hills Kiwanis Club, I could literally see the eyebrows of successful business and professional men in the audience climb up their foreheads, but two men in attendance that day didn't laugh. One was a manager of a small employment agency and the other was a self-styled poet. Today the first man is head of a nationwide employment service with branches in many cities and his daily income is still climbing in a most fantastic manner. The second man spoke to me after the meeting and among other things he said, "I want to be Poet Laureate of California. Do you think I can make it?" My reply: "If you have what it takes, yes." This man looked me squarely in the eye and replied, "I believe I have."

Five years later, almost to the day, this determined person sent me a telegram from the State Capitol in Sacramento, saying, "Unanimous approval rules committee. Waiting in Assembly for final passage." And so it was that on June 10, 1953, Gordon W. Norris was made the fourth Poet Laureate of California in a joint session of the legislature—simply because he believed in himself so strongly that he never quit trying.

On another occasion I was having lunch with an aspiring motion picture star in the commissary at Universal Studios in Hollywood. The girl was young and lovely with an accent that was heavily West Indian and she had a driving ambition. She knew that to reach stardom in a town that overflowed with beautiful women, something more than just beauty was necessary. She had it—an unusual idea. She said to me, "I believe people of all ages will like fairy tales. I want to do something like Arabian Nights."

At the time I treated the idea lightly, but in less than two years I had to eat crow. When the picture *Arabian Nights* was shown to the press, Maria Montez couldn't resist winking impishly at me as she walked from the studio preview theatre. From that moment on, whenever a wild idea was broached to me, I wisely kept my comments to myself.

A Bonanza From "Dogs"

Way back in 1919 an enterprising haberdasher by the name of Walter Nordlinger startled the merchandising world half out of its stolid wits. The town was Washington, D.C., and the time was shortly after the close of World War I, when business could have been better. In this situation, Nordlinger had a problem. Too much window exposure had faded some of his stock of expensive shirts. At the asking price no one was interested, so this man put a quick sale tag of 50¢ on them and on that day custom was born.

Since that inauspicious beginning, customers from miles around Washington look forward to the huge Washington's Birthday sales, because now everybody gets into the act. All that is needed to unload huge quantities of odds and ends of left-over items is to put a price on them. At first the Better Business Bureau took a dim view of the situation, but time and success soon softened this opposition although they admit that some merchants take advantage of the buying spirit of enthusiastic customers to palm off shoddy goods.

Be that as it may, there are few complaints. Most persons know that they get what they pay for—and the chesterfield coat that sold for less than ten dollars still comes close to looking like its original value of $125.00.

Even a Rose Can Make You Rich

Not too many persons know that if you can create a new type of rose the United States Patent Office will protect your horticultural product with an exclusive grant to market for a period of seventeen years. And that isn't all. Should you christen your rose by an unusual or exotic name, or name it after a famous personality, the title you have selected for your creation can be registered and thus protect your idea permanently.

During the years the list of rose names included in the International Rose Register has climbed steadily until now the total is nearing the ten thousand mark. Quite an achievement for a mere flower.

Anything Goes

The reason I cite these several commonplace ideas is for the sole purpose of making it clear that anything goes. There isn't a single everyday item that you can name that doesn't contain the elements of great fortune. All you have to do is think beyond the obvious. You can start your prospecting venture by asking yourself a few simple questions about the idea, product or device that you are contemplating. Consider the following:

1. Will an interest-compelling name help?
2. Is there a new or different use for this item lurking here unseen?
3. Could this idea be adapted and used in some other field?

In my talks to service clubs and civic groups covering my favorite topic of innovation I like to emphasize these points. Naturally enough, this is a challenge that is frequently accepted by persons in the audience. Often the product or service of a questioner will be mentioned. On more than one occasion this completely inadequate, off-the-cuff brainstorming will cause more than one person to comment, "Well, what do you know about this!"

At other times someone present will hand me an ordinary product and ask, "What can you do with this?" During one question-and-answer period, one of the men present handed me a tenpenny nail. This item is about as low in the scale of commonplace things as you can go since it was one of the very early inventions of man, but a sudden inspiration hit me. "What," I asked, "would you think of a nail that would do so-and-so?"

"Mister," this chap retorted, "if you can do that, our firm alone will make you a millionaire." As I am writing this, I can't tell you how it is going to turn out, but I am presently directing all twelve of my precious mind powers to solving the problem. And I have the strongest feeling it can be done.

HOW TO SPOT A "SLEEPER"

The man or woman who is always thinking like a millionaire does three things as a matter of habit:

1. He looks beyond the obvious, even in ordinary things.
2. He learns to estimate the value of any item over and above its commonplace appearance or usage.
3. He learns to raise his sights. That is, he looks over all the routine outlets for the item, and then lets his money consciousness take a broad, high look for new, and perhaps completely different sources of interest.

"Getting a Corner" on Old Street Corner Signs

Does that heading sound goofy? Wait until you have read the story. It seems that one Libby O'Brien accomplished this very thing. It all happened in such a prosy manner that the good lady almost passed up a tidy fortune.

One day Miss O'Brien was traveling to her home in Old Greenwich, Connecticut, when she happened to glance out of the window of the New Haven train and saw a huge pile of old street signs piled up in a vacant lot in the Bronx. For almost half a century New York had marked its street intersections with big iron signs, painted blue, with white lettering. Late in the fall of the previous year, the city began to replace the ancient markers with smaller yellow signs with black letters, and the old signs had to be dumped. Here they were in a vacant lot. The pile grew and grew until the unsightly heap caught the attention of a fast-thinking woman.

Early the next morning, Libby O'Brien went searching. Before too long she was directed to the city's department of traffic. To her inquiry, "Are the signs for sale?" she got a terse retort, "Why not? Make us a bid." And this she did. Right out of her head she picked the figure of $478.00—probably because that was the amount she had tucked away in her cookie jar. At any rate her bid was accepted, especially since no one else seemed to be interested. With the signs now her legal property, she was faced with a moving and marketing problem in that order. The city had given her thirty days to remove the "junk."

The little lady tackled her problem with imagination. She began parading her wares through Grand Central Station, with gratifying results. Her pile of 10,000 old signs began to disappear rapidly at prices ranging from ten to fifty dollars. Not bad for a quick look out of a train window.

And Then There Is "Space"

With all of a thousand pieces of hardware floating around "up there" some hard-thinking person is going to come up with a salvaging idea one of these days and become a millionaire overnight, especially since more junk is going into orbit each week. Recovery of these floating monstrosities isn't the only source of wealth from the space program; imaginative firms all over the nation are now working on kits, tools, and devices that will serve to make the "moon project" more rewarding, or other expeditions into outer space more revealing.

You Can "Think and Grow Rich," but First You Have to Put On Your "Million Dollar Glasses"

Once as I traveled into Hollywood from my home in Riverside, I donned my rose-colored glasses just for fun. The trip is only about sixty miles, but in that brief passage I counted nine potential money-making opportunities that were apparently going begging for lack of a taker. This lamentable situation could only derive from one thing. The men and women driving into town were too concerned with the problems of the day, such as home, business, or who said what to whom, instead of looking for chances to make money that seem to be everywhere. I am quite positive that if the situation I have described prevails in Southern California, a comparatively new settlement, there are 10,000 more opportunities in older sections of the country—like the street signs rusting away on a vacant lot in the Bronx.

THERE IS A MONEY-MAKING REASON

For every idea, device, or product that is created, there is always the potential of a thousand variations. It is up to you to examine with imagination commonplace products or services.

Every time you open the door on anything new or different or expand the utility of an ordinary item, you are opening up vistas of accomplishment that can extend down the brightly lit "corridors of time." On the face of it this might appear just a little too poetic, but the truth of the matter is plain. Like space, there is no limit to the future.

There is only one word of caution. Within the context of the guideline you are now reading, it is quite essential that you build your road to great riches one block at a time, so that the next step you take is the cement that binds your own avenue to wealth together as solidly as the Appian Way that joined the vast Roman Empire.

SUMMARY

1. The first move any individual must make in order to get in the white water flow of the success cycle is to become an outstanding expert in something.

2. The next move is to grab a brass ring—that is, pick an idea, an item, a product, or a service, either lay or professional, and find something in that single thing to seize on mentally— because what you select for special interest is a freeway ticket to great accomplishment, regardless of what sparks your attention.

3. Should you need guidance in determining what to concentrate on, begin to sort, choose and eliminate until you have sharpened the natural tool of selective curiosity to a razor-thin edge, and then you will be able to pick that which is good for you.

4. When you find what you want, direct your attention to the *five moves* that will provide you with a permanent place on the crest of the success cycle and ride it out.

5. And remember always, even the most commonplace ideas, events, or products contain the seeds of great fortune. All you have to do is to wear your rose-colored glasses and look beyond the obvious.

How to Persuade People to Do Just What You Want Them to Do*

10

Perhaps the most sought-after job skill today . . . and thus the skill that can earn the most money for you . . . is the ability to make others want to take action. If you're a supervisor you'll be promoted faster if you can motivate your employees to do better work . . . if you're a salesman you'll earn high commissions if you make customers want to buy . . . and if you're a schoolteacher you'll get a job in the best school system if you earn a reputation for making children want to learn.

I don't think this ability is in such demand because only a few people have it . . . I believe anyone can be a successful motivator. It's true that this ability comes naturally to some. But even if you're not one of the naturally gifted ones, there's no reason why you can't easily learn and use the few basic techniques that will make you an instinctive people motivator . . . and the key to making others want to act lies in the conversational skills and knowledge presented in this chapter.

THE MODERN WAY TO GET THINGS DONE

As you know, nobody willingly lets others order him around . . . employees won't jump just because a boss commands it . . . nor does a

---

*James A. Morris, Jr., *The Art of Conversation: The Magic Key to Personal and Social Popularity* (Englewood Cliffs, N.J.: Prentice-Hall, Inc., 1976).

teenager "snap to" simply because his father orders it. People want to think for themselves. In a climate like this, you have to get things done the modern way . . . by motivating others . . . by making others want to do what you want them to. The way to get yourself started using this modern conversational technique is first by grasping these few basic principles:

- People do what they do because they feel comfortable acting that way . . . when someone's happy with the way things are, he has no reason to change. But if this same person becomes unhappy with his current state of affairs, then he'll feel uncomfortable.
- People don't like feeling uncomfortable . . . so, when they feel this way, they're open to suggestions that will help them feel happy again.
- When they learn of a new way to behave that removes their discomfort, they'll gladly change their actions. They'll be motivated . . . they'll want to act in the new way.

Now let's see how these principles work in everyday situations:

Suppose you're a supervisor and you have an employee, Johnny Treble, who talks too much. In fact, he enjoys talking so much that he dominates every conversation he's in. During one of his monologues, you observe him from afar and notice that Larry Rhodes walks away from Johnny with a disgusted look on his face. You chat with Larry for a minute, then approach Johnny and remark, "Boy, Larry seems angry about something. Don't know what he meant, but he mumbled something about not being able to get a word in edgewise."

This is bound to make Johnny feel uncomfortable . . . he knows that Larry was just with him, so Larry must be angry about the way he acted.

As soon as you notice Johnny's discomfort, you might follow with a second remark, "You know Larry is a great conversationalist. He really knows how to listen."

If Johnny has any sensitivity at all, he'll catch what you're really saying: the suggestion you put between the lines of your conversation . . . "You'll keep Larry as a friend if you simply talk a little less and listen a little more." And, since Johnny is feeling uncomfortable, he'll want to change his way of acting . . . he'll want to remove his discomfort by being careful not to talk too much in the future.

Though all motivating conversations don't go as smoothly as this one, it does illustrate the modern way to get things done . . . first, make the other fellow feel uncomfortable about his current actions . . . second, show him a new and better way to act that will remove his discomfort . . . third, stand aside and let him change of his own free will. These principles can easily be put to work by following the conversational steps described in the rest of this chapter.

As you use these steps, you'll begin developing the persuasive power that makes your conversations pay off. Perhaps when you first read them, they may seem a bit involved . . . but as you work with them, they'll seem very natural. Before you know it they'll become a habit. This is good . . . the power of your persuasive conversation will grow as you use these steps more and more. And the more often you use them, the better you will become at motivating others; it won't be long before you'll have the most sought-after skill on the job market today . . . the job skill that has earned promotion after promotion for many conversationalists.

THE SECRETS OF GETTING THROUGH
TO OTHERS

Do you remember how Boy Scouts are taught to make a fire without using matches? First, they cut a pile of dry wood shavings, then they strike a flint until a spark falls onto the shavings. Finally they blow on the spark until the shavings start to blaze.

Getting through to other people is much like this fire-starting project. First you prepare a "bed" of attention, then you strike a spark and conversationally fan it until it creates a blaze of interest.

Let's continue the comparison between fire starting and conversation . . . a spark will burst into fire when the wood shavings are dry and have not absorbed a lot of dampness . . . similarly a blaze of interest is created when the other person's mind is "dry," when it is not absorbed with its own thoughts or emotions. Here are ways to help you break down the two most common mind absorbers that prevent you from getting the other fellow's attention:

Breaking Through Preoccupations

If a supervisor is busy planning the production sequence for some rush parts, he won't be interested in listening to his foreman's vacation scheduling problems. But his attention focuses fast if the same foreman bursts into his office exclaiming, "Our turret lathe just broke down . . . our whole production line will have to stop unless you order one of the maintenance men to drop a routine job and fix the lathe fast." Moral of this example: When someone is wrestling with his own problems he won't pay attention to you . . . unless what you have to say is more important than his thoughts.

Another way to penetrate a preoccupied mind is to help the other fellow solve his problem. Say, for example, you walk into Bill's office and notice him studying a map.

"Planning a trip?" you ask.

"Yeh, got to drive to Buffalo tomorrow."

"I made that trip last month and the AAA suggested I go this way," you advise, as your finger traces the fastest route. At this point Bill's mind is free and ready to turn its attention to what you have to say.

Relieving the Other Person's Tensions

When someone's nerves are tied up in knots, his mind will be tied up too. So to get his attention you first must relieve his tensions. Here are two techniques I've found helpful:

- Set an example by keeping yourself relaxed. A quiet, soft voice . . . slow and deliberate movements . . . a calm attentiveness toward his personal needs and feelings . . . actions like these create a relaxed atmosphere in which he can unwind.

- Keep the conversation centered on topics that are safe. Don't discuss a subject that may aggravate or excite him. Do talk about relaxing subjects like his hobby or his plans for the coming weekend. There's one exception to this technique: if he is emotionally up-tight about something, then it's often best to let him talk it out. Once he's had a chance to vent his emotions, he should quiet down and give you his attention.

Making Him Feel Appreciated . . .

Another time-proven way you can gain someone's attention is to let the other fellow know you appreciate him . . . that you value him as a person. Once he senses this high regard, he'll usually show interest in you and what you have to say. Naturally, your feelings towards him must be sincere . . . you'll lose both his attention and his respect at the slightest hint of falseness. Here are some simple techniques our friend, conversationalist George Reade, uses to make another person feel appreciated and thereby to gain his attention:

- Show consideration for his feelings.
- Don't critize him or embarrass him in any way.
- Listen attentively and sincerely when he speaks.
- Never dismiss any remarks of his as unimportant . . . when he comments on something, think about it and then respond appropriately.
- Recognize his strong points by deciding which of his personal traits he is most proud of, and by showing him that you recognize these traits by comments such as

"What a memory, Wish mine were as good."
"How do you keep coming up with such good jokes?"
"Boy, you learn fast."

Preventing Him from Tuning You Out . . .

Attention is an elusive thing; just as soon as you think you have captured it, it can slip away from you. That's why I always keep alert for these warning signs that the other fellows attention is drifting:

Restlessness. You know what these signs are like . . . he shifts uneasily in his chair . . . his hands fidget nervously with a nearby object . . . you get an inner feeling that he's itching to jump up and run away from you. These warning signs tell you that either he isn't interested in what you're discussing or you're saying or doing something that is annoying him. To cure his restlessness first decide what is turning him off, and then change either the topic or your conversational style.

Repeated questions. If he re-asks questions you've already answered, you know that one of the following is happening:

- His mind is starting to wander since he obviously wasn't paying attention to what you said before. If this is the case, then work on regaining his attention.
- He didn't understand your first answer. If this is so, then re-explain your answer in different words, taking enough time to be sure he understands.
- He disagreed with your first answer. The problem of disagreement is so important that we'll talk more about it later in this chapter.

Unrelated statements. Let's say that your company has invented a new style of widget that you think will give you some manufacturing problems. You start to discuss these with Terry when he interrupts, "How can I handle my current work with that broken down lathe I've got?" His remark is completely unrelated to widgets; he isn't ready yet to talk about them. So change the topic . . . discuss how Terry can either repair or replace his old lathe . . . then once this problem is off his mind, he'll be willing to turn his attention toward discussing widgets.

You get through to another person by first clearing his mind of preoccupations and emotional tensions, next by making him feel appreciated as a person, and finally by taking care that he doesn't tune you out. Follow these techniques and you can open up his mind to what you have to say and thereby start a productive, motivating conversation.

HOW TO PLANT YOUR TARGET IN HIS MIND

Now that you have captured his attention and interest, you're ready to take the first step in motivating him into action . . . you can conversationally plant the key idea in his mind that there is a better way of acting than the way he's acting now.

For example, let's say that you manage a large department. One of your employees, Sam, is giving you a problem . . . though his work output is good, his work area is always sloppy. Your target: Motivate him into wanting to keep a clean work area. Thus, you must plant the idea in his mind that proper appearance is as important as work output. Here are three conversational techniques you can use to do this:

Using a Long Established "Idea Planter"

Remember how you learned math and spelling back in school . . . you repeated the principles over and over until they became part of you. Educators discovered long ago that repetition is a vital link in the learning process. And since you want Sam to learn that appearance is important, repetition will also be one of your main working tools. You won't use repetition in a nagging way; rather you'll drop subtle hints from time to time.

When you walk by Sam's work area you could remark, "Your work area looks unorganized . . . having any troubles?" When he answers, "No troubles. Everything's going fine," you can close the conversation casually with, "Glad to hear it. I thought maybe you were too busy solving a problem to have any time for cleanup."

Then about a week later you could remark, "The big boss came to work before starting time today and noticed how messy your work area was. He asked me if you were falling behind in your work." This remark reinforces your original comment and adds the extra impact that the big boss is also concerned about neat appearances.

Guiding His Thinking with a Teacher's Technique

Right after telling him the big boss's remark, you immediately move into another familiar method used by teachers—the question technique—by asking him, "Why do you think the big boss feels that a messy work area means that something is going wrong?" Don't answer the question for him; make him think it through and decide for himself that workers are often judged on the appearance of their work area, especially by someone who doesn't know the details of the worker's recent performance.

By using questions you are forcing Sam to tell you why it's a good idea to keep a clean work area. This technique is much more to your advantage than lecturing Sam on the virtues of cleanliness. When you lecture, Sam will feel that the idea is being forced on him . . . that he has no say in the matter . . . and he'll end up resenting you. But when you ask questions Sam will feel that he came up with the idea . . . he was the one who said that a messy work area reflects badly on him. You'll have planted your idea in Sam's mind without arousing his resentment.

A Salesman's Method for Assuring that Ideas Stay Planted

Once your question-teaching has led Sam to say that cleanliness is important, then congratulate him for realizing this fact. Use a proven sales technique . . . lead him into thinking that the idea was his in the first place. "Yes, I think you've hit on the answer. The big boss must think that anyone who has a messy work area isn't on top of his job." Keep Sam talking and thinking about this discovery "he made." In this way you'll be using persuasive conversation to plant your idea firmly in his mind . . . you'll be making him aware of a new way of working without getting him angry with you for "forcing" him to change.

TECHNIQUES THAT GAIN ACCEPTANCE
FOR YOUR IDEA

Next you want him to accept that the new way of acting is better than what he's doing. This is where the fireworks can begin . . . people don't like to change so they naturally resist new ways of doing things. But as Sam becomes dissatisfied with his current actions, he'll feel an inner conflict . . . this works to your advantage. Since people don't like conflict, they run away from it. And if the idea you conversationally planted removes this conflict, he'll want to accept the idea. So keep talking persuasively about the idea, keep motivating him into acting in the new way. You want him to become so completely involved with the new idea that he finally accepts it as his own and acts on it.

Avoiding False Acceptance

Be suspicious if Sam immediately agrees to change his habits and work neatly . . . people just don't accept new ways of acting that fast. Ask yourslef, "Is Sam telling me what I want to hear without really

meaning what he says?" Many people play the game of false acceptance . . . their reasoning is, "Why let myself in for a lot of unpleas-
antness? I'll agree to whatever he wants and act as if I've changed for a
while. Then when he has forgotten about the incident, I'll go back to
my old ways."

Of course, two can play this game. What you do is be sure you
don't forget. When you see him start to slide back into his old habits,
step in fast and reapply your motivating conversation.

Drawing Out His Objections

Since you know that people resist new ideas, why not draw this
resistance out into the open where you can handle it conversationally
in a positive way? Here are two key ways to do this:

- Keep asking questions that encourage him to voice his feelings about the new idea.
- Keep yourself under control and don't argue against his objections or try to prove him wrong.

This positive approach helps you because it keeps him open
minded! If you start to attack his objections, the other fellow may
correctly think to himself, "Why bother talking; he's not interested in
my feelings, he just wants me to agree with him." He'll then withdraw
within himself. To prevent this, just take the time to consider each of
his remarks. For example, here are some of the objections Sam could
raise about your new idea:

Sam:	"If I have to keep my work area spotless, I'll never be able to keep up my work output."
You:	That's a point . . . the time you spend in housecleaning is that much less time you have for doing the work itself."
Sam:	"I just can't waste time. I'm paid to get the work out, not be a janitor."
You:	"You're darned right it takes time. I'm glad you realize that."

Later, after all his objections have been aired, you can counter
them with persuasive conversation such as: "Although cleaning up

takes time, a neat work area allows you to work more efficiently. I'll bet you can keep your area clean and turn out the work as well. Why not give it a try?"

Deciding if His Objections Are Emotional or Logical

As he voices his objections, the key questions to ask yourself are these: "Is he overreacting to the change I suggested? Is he being too emotional in his resistance? If you answer these questions "no," chances are his objections are logical ones. If you answer "yes," then he is reacting emotionally.

Here are some additional questions that help you spot emotional reactions:

- Is his voice higher pitched than usual? Is it louder? Is he speaking at a faster pace than is normal?
- Is he jumping quickly from one objection to another as if he were trying to overpower your idea by the sheer number of things he can find wrong with it?
- Is he stubbornly holding to his previous thinking and refusing even to consider your idea?
- Is he bringing up objections that are unrelated to your idea? Does he seem to be hiding his real objections?

In the example given above, odds are that Sam's first statement is a logical objection . . . note how Sam presents his opinion in a straightforward manner. The second comment, on the other hand, has the outward appearance of an emotional reaction.

How to Handle Logical Objections

The easiest way to counter a logical objection is with facts and common sense. But first be sure that his objection has been brought fully into the open. Going back to Sam's first statement, you might get him to expand on his objection by asking, "It's true that cleaning up takes time, but why do you think that work output would fall if you worked in a neater way?"

If he answers, "Obviously, when I'm cleaning, I'm not producing," you have a perfect chance to help him see his job differently.

You could explain first that the amount he produces is dependent on how efficiently he works, not on how much time he spends. Second, you could conversationally point out how a neat work area helps him organize the job better, thus allowing him to work more efficiently. The end result, you could explain, "is both a cleaner work area and a higher output."

How to Handle Emotional Objections

Patience and a listening ear are your two major weapons when you face an emotional objector.

The first thing you should do is encourage him to sound off as much as he wants to. Just listen quietly and sympathetically until the full force of his emotion is spent. As mentioned earlier in this chapter, you can't get through to someone who is emotionally up-tight.

After he quiets down is the time to make him realize that he's taking an unreasonable position. Do this by discussing his comments calmly, not by attacking his objections or accusing him of being emotional. Your chances of success are greater if you can get him to admit to himself that he's being unreasonable.

Back to Sam's second comment, here are some ways you can respond conversationally to his emotional outburst:

- "You feel that we need to hire a janitor to help keep your work area clean! If we did hire one, we'd have to prove that your output would increase enough to cover the extra salary we'd have to pay. Do you think this would happen?
- "I notice that the other fellows keep their work areas clean . . . is their output lower than yours?"

As you calmly and logically discuss his objections, he will begin to feel uncomfortable . . . he'll begin to see that his objections are not supported by fact. He'll begin to feel a bit foolish and, therefore, will start to change his attitude.

During your motivating conversation, keep projecting a sincere interest in the points he raises, and keep showing respect for him as a person . . . never belittle him or laugh at his statements, rather listen to him with the same honest concern that you'd expect from others if you were the objector.

Finally, as his emotions start to fade, help him move from emotional spoutings to logical objections. Once he reaches the point of logic, your chances of motivating him are much greater.

You conversationally motivate someone when you cause him to accept that a new way of acting is better than his way. And since no one likes to change, he'll resist your idea. Bring this resistance out into the open by getting him to voice his objections, then calmly discuss the merits and demerits of his objections. As you do this, he'll see your idea in its best light . . . you will gradually lead him into accepting your idea.

HOW TO KEEP HIM GOING UNTIL
THE JOB IS FINISHED

Once he has been conversationally motivated to your idea, getting him to change often requires no more effort than simply asking him to take appropriate action. In salesmanship this is called "asking for the order." And as any sales manager can tell you, this is the area where many salesmen fall down . . . they present a beautiful case for their product . . . they show the other fellow what he'll gain from buying the product . . . then they stop.

Returning to the example of your employee, Sam, suppose you had gone through each of the preceding steps. You had cleared his mind of distractions . . . you had planted your target in his mind and handled all objections . . . you had led him into accepting the idea as his own. Yet you still haven't "asked for the order." True, he may have agreed, "I think it's a good idea to clean up my work area." But when? Tomorrow . . . next week . . . next month . . . next year? Human inertia being what it is, if you stop your motivating conversation at this point, he probably won't start cleaning until next year. So ask for the order, "That's a great idea you have, Sam. Why don't you start cleaning first thing tomorrow? Before you know it, you'll be finished and ready to start in on your regular work again."

This conversational step is vital; if you want to motivate someone, you must ask him to take action. Don't just present a case and sit there expecting him to take the initiative. Rather, brace up and simply yet firmly ask the other fellow to do what you want him to do. Only when he responds to your request will you have completed your job of conversationally motivating him to take action.

If he refuses to act, you know that you haven't satisfied all of his objections. So return to the previous step and get him discussing your idea once more. Ask questions that encourage him to bring up any objections he didn't voice earlier. Then handle these new objections in the same way you handled his original ones. Once this is done, again tell him what you want him to do. Chances are that he'll go along with you this time.

Now that you've conversationally motivated him into acting in a new way, everything will go along fine for a while. But then the original enthusiasm you created for the new target may begin to wane . . . you may find him slipping back into his old ways. This is the time to follow through, to keep him motivated by using these proven techniques—remind him of the need for change, and make him happy about his change.

Reminding Him of the Need for Change

This technique is similar to the repetition technique except that you're now doing it after change rather than before it. Your target is to assure that he stays motivated, to keep him convinced that he was right in making the change in the first place. You don't have to comment as often as when you were motivating him to change . . . just speak up every now and then with comments such as:

- "Certainly looks like you're on top of your job."
- "The big boss commented today about the change that's occurred in your work area. He's pleased."

Making Him Happy About His Change

When someone does a good job he likes to be congratulated. It's only human. So handle him the way you'd like to be treated by praising him for changing:

"Certainly have to take my hat off to you—the way you keep your area neat, yet still turn out the work . . ."

Reward him with a compliment every now and then, and you'll keep his motivation fired up and prevent him from slipping back into his old habits.

Keeping Your Interest Active . . .

You'll keep his interest in the change alive by keeping yours alive . . . by reminding him of the need to act differently and by congratulating him on his successful change. Give him the total credit for changing, but make sure he knows you are aware of his accomplishment.

Showing that you're sincerely interested in the other fellow and following the actions described in this chapter will dramatically increase your ability to persuade others to adopt your point of view. And by remaining actively interested in them after you have persuaded them conversationally, you'll not only assure that they stay changed, but you'll also earn their respect and friendship.

How to Come out on Top in Every People-Handling Situation You Will Ever Face*

No matter how successful you were in improving another's attitude, don't let his enthusiasm die by doing nothing else. Keep moving! You can make one of a dozen moves that will make him act. It's like selling: the salesman makes it easy for the prospect to say "I'll buy." Make it easy for the person you're dealing with to say "I'll do," or better still, to do it.

Many principles will help you maintain momentum. Some that you will want to learn and put into practice are:

1. Schedule details that make it easy for the other person to act.
2. Get him to see action as his job.
3. Appeal to his desires.
4. Let him change his mind.
5. Handle the key person right.
6. Make the most of functional authority.
7. Keep communications open for future action.
8. Stir enthusiasm.

---

*A. G. Strickland, *How to Get Action: Key to Successful Management* (Englewood Cliffs, N. J.: Prentice-Hall, Inc., 1975).

Let's take a look at other managers' successful application of these and other sure-fire principles.

SCHEDULING DETAILS SO IT'S EASY
FOR OTHERS TO ACT

There were 39 high-ranking people assembled in the room for a one-day conference and Jim Gilpin, manager of Industrial Planning, was in charge. The whole program was a gamble: if it worked, it would be a great success; if it didn't, heads would roll. High-level people from many related companies who came to the conference were going to be treated as if they were in a conference to get action and they would *have* to participate. Almost from the start they would be broken into small groups to discuss the major problem. Beforehand several managers said, "But you don't marshall people of this level," "They may be embarrassed," and "They may refuse." Rather than quibble, Jim made the choice—that he'd get great or zero results. He selected the best, most spacious room, set up individual tables for six or seven, and put pencils and pads at each place (capitalizing on an irresistible urge to pick up a pencil and doodle which can be transformed into involvement). Coffee was available on entry. The whole atmosphere from the entrance into the room was one of participation. A few minutes were allowed for conversation at the tables.

After a short but very proper welcome, Jim presented the problem and told them, "You will discuss this at your table and define obstacles to solving the problem. You will have 15 minutes." Jim then left the room. There was an electrifying silence as it dawned on these high-level gentlemen that he meant business: he was in control and he expected action.

After 30 shattering seconds of silence, they plunged into the discussion and continued with enthusiasm the whole day. They loved being asked to participate, and the confidence of expected action was in the atmosphere. Jim knew how to schedule details so that a little action led to a little more. Try the same with both your high-level and low-level people. Schedule details to facilitate their action.

HOW TO MAKE THE ACTION OR
DECISION SEEM SMALL

Salesmen know how to substitute a small choice for a large one; a minor detail for a large decision; a matter of filling in information on a form—anything to keep the person from having to sit and wrestle with a major decision and come up with a negative. Take a step or two in the direction of the desired action and make it easy for the other person to complete it.

In a leading manufacturing firm, eleven departments, ranging from Tool Design to Accounts Payable, were to receive presentations honoring them for good work. This meant that the top executive, Ila Smith, would have to make many presentations. Joe Daley, Industrial Relations manager, had twice set up appointments with him to discuss details but both meetings were postponed. Finally Doug, another manager, suggested, "Listen, when you described the idea you heard Mr. Smith say that he liked it. Why don't you:

1. Call his secretary and see if he has the needed time,
2. Block out his calendar,
3. Schedule the presentations, and
4. Call the photographer.

"Then when you see him, you can say, here is the plan. If he doesn't want to do it, he'll say so. Otherwise it'll be ready to go, and think of all the time you'll save him and yourself."

Doug showed Joe how to make it easy for the chief executive to act—and he did.

Why not make the decision and allow time for the other fellow to reverse it if necessary?

At another time, the top man handed a proposal to Joe and requested that he look it over. "We'll discuss plans later," he said. Joe, upon seeing the proposal, had very definite ideas as to the action needed, but was afraid that the boss wouldn't agree. To sell his idea the easy way, Joe composed a telegram outlining the action and presented it to his boss.

"Shall I send it?" he asked. It was so easy to do that his boss said "Yes" immediately. Joe scheduled action and he got it. Do as much as you can toward action and it will seem small for the other person to complete. Action-getting has paid off for Joe. He's since moved from Industrial Relations Manager to Division Manager for Labor Relations and Employee Services, with twice the employees and a good increase in salary.

HOW TO KEEP THE RELATIONSHIP
SMOOTH FOR FUTURE ACTION

Keep the relationship amicable so that you can deal effectively with the man next time. Barney, a manager in an office near me will do anything to get results—*anything,* no matter who gets sore about it! But next time around, Barney won't get cooperation because he has completely disrupted lines of communication. Get results, yes—but remember you've got to deal with people again. Each time you have to "push" someone to get results:

- Thank the man for his help.
- Allow him to recover his ego if you push him very far.
- Allow him to win some points and be right to some extent.
- Let him feel good about the result even if you had to lead him to it.

Dwayne Young, manager of an extrusion department, had to get Bud Nolan, a representative from one of the service organizations, to devote time to a project. Dwayne forced Bud to act. He plainly told Bud he was being lax, and called several times to remind Bud of the requirements. He would not let him off the hook. In the long run, Bud did it, but he would not speak to Dwayne for several months. Dwayne then had to spend time "mending the fence." After about a half year, Bud started speaking to him and gradually reestablished a good working relationship.

There are many ways to force people without pushing them too far too fast. Keep ego in mind and gauge the push in the light of future relations. Don't disrupt them for all time.

John Ransom, assistant production manager, held a meeting of machine shop managers in a large manufacturing company. They desperately needed better service from the maintenance department, so they also invited the maintenance manager. Before the meeting John warned the other members, "Don't come down on the man personally. Don't go overboard in criticizing maintenance. Keep it on a level of asking for his help." That they did, and the maintenance manager worked hard to help clear up the situation.

Every time we deal with a person, our relationship either improves or deteriorates. It never stays the same. Leave it improved if possible.

HOW TO USE "AGGRESSIVE" PATIENCE TO KEEP THINGS MOVING

John Tanner, an assistant to the president of a production company, needed to keep a close surveillance on the quality of supervision.

John had an idea for a company-wide supervisory improvement program. It needed approval by a council—at least tacit approval. The management development department had the wherewithal to plan and implement. It would be appropriate for management development to come up with the idea in the first place—for the council to recommend and approve it.

John had to plant the seeds in meetings with the group and the council. The management development group had to be challenged although they had a responsibility, as a group of experts, to originate the proposal. A meeting was called and the need was discussed, without stating a solution. At first there was a dull thud as members of the group brought out all negatives. The group considered and considered and one man ventured that "We should consider company-wide supervisory improvement, but it will have to be done immediately and that means improving 1,500 supervisors." He was told, "That's the right track, but how can we do it?" The group decided it could be done by setting up small groups of supervisors plant-wide to meet on a regular basis with a chairman. How could they be gotten to consider the topic of supervision without their being preached to? They could start by examining the labor relations problems in their groups. This could lead to looking at some other human relations problems. They then planned the mechanics of the session.

This was exactly what John wanted implemented in the first place, but *they thought of it* and they would make it work. Meanwhile, the same process went on in the council so that they recommended the same thing.

It took five times as long to arrive at the plan, but it became five times as easy to put into practice because it had been run through their thinking. Be patient and help *them* arrive at what *you* want to do. Eisenhower said, "Leadership is getting a man to do what *you* want him to do because *he* wants to do it." It takes aggressive patience to work through people, but the results are worth it.

HOW YOU CAN GAIN COOPERATION BY APPEALING TO SOMETHING THE OTHER PERSON WANTS

There'd been bad blood between the shop managers in Catesville Mall and G. G. MacLane, the real estate manager who owned it. Constant bickering about everything from Christmas tree lights to who would connect the fountain in the Plaza had caused a complete breach. Someone had to move if the Mall was to be promoted and business brought in. The managers organized and suggested hiring a lawyer to do it for them. Warren Strand, owner of a gift shop, said, "Wait! That real estate company is basically honest. They just constantly fail to act. I have a plan." Warren called on G. G. MacLane. After listening to everything from "I got stuck at Christmas" to the preamble to the Magna Carta he stated, "Mac, your company will make an override from our sales. You need increased traffic in this shopping center. If a store fails, you must face an empty building or more expensive selling. So you stand to gain as much as we do by this promotion. Let's get together and work out a plan to 'sell' the center." MacLane said, "O.K. I'll meet you Monday." *Fait accompli!* Why? Warren considered what Mac wanted. That's a basic principle in getting action—appeal to something the other person wants. The other merchants think Warren is the smartest man on two feet when it comes to getting things done.

Too often the intense desire to get results will cause us to think only of what we want. What about the other man? He has his own wants and when he moves it will be to satisfy some of them. Why not consider these carefully and help him satisfy one or more, and in the process get results?

USING THE DESIRES THAT PEOPLE HAVE IN COMMON

People often say, "I work with a bunch of artists. They think differently;" or "I work with men in production. They think differently." All of us have common wants. Suppose we consider these wants. Check with any of the authorities—Freud, Adler, or William James—and you will find on the top of their list of desires of every man a desire for *appreciation,* or *feeling of importance* or *recognition.* Call it what you will, it is still the self-satisfaction of being important. If you consider when it comes to changing things that everybody has this built-in desire, you can utilize it and get better results.

Dan Bruno owns and manages an art store. When he got started, he needed a great deal of help because he wasn't sure exactly what would sell. He saw that he needed the support of the art teachers at three high schools in the county, and of a couple of dozen artists in the local art colony.

Dan planned a private sneak preview and coffee for his store and invited 50 to 100 key people. This was before the store opened for business. He asked each to jot down suggestions for the store. The artists were pleased, the high school teachers were pleased and, best of all, Dan was pleased. He had made them feel important and had done it sincerely. They won't trade anywhere else. In fact, the teachers now call him before they start a class to see that he is stocked up.

The key was that Dan appealed to their importance. It is a desire we have in common. So if you are ever in doubt as to what moves the other man, keep this in mind. It can get results.

HELPING HIM SEE THE ACTION YOU WANT AS A PART OF HIS JOB

Harvey Daleman was head of a finance department. Tom Coyle, his assistant finance manager called a meeting of representatives on an issue that was part of their job obligation. "I had 12 of 18 repre-

sentatives present," Harvey fumed. One third of his committee repre-
senting all finance departments didn't feel it was worthwhile to attend
the meeting and didn't even feel compelled to tell him why.

Tom complained, "Enthusiasm is waning in our organization."
Why not? He was the culprit. It seemed that Tom had communicated
the unimportance of the meeting; he had communicated a "why
bother" or an "if you don't have anything else to do" attitude to his
people, so you couldn't blame them.

When Harvey questioned Tom about this sort of attendance,
Tom said, "Aw, you always shoot for 100 percent."

Harvey roared, "You're darned right! Every man who doesn't
attend the meeting after he's committed is expected to have an A-1
excuse or a written note from his mother. His presence is needed or he
wouldn't be on the committee. If he's got a thousand other things to
do, don't ask him to serve on a committee for kicks. If he's needed, he's
needed; so he's expected to attend."

After this lecture from Harvey, Tom went back and wrote a
memo to all involved managers: "Your man will be there, or I should
know why, or change men." At the next meeting he had to send out for
chairs.

It's critical that the people working for you understand that you're
not buying their time, but productivity of some sort—the results of
applying their time. To assure that your organization gets what it
deserves you must make any one who deals with it feel the same. Let
the individual know what action is expected as a part of his job.

THE SECRET OF GETTING ENTHUSIASM

Roy Stratford, production manager of an assembly plant, was
having a bad time with one of his men who criticized the electrical
wiring department. Everything that came out was wrong, or he didn't
like it for some reason. Roy put him in that department as manager
and before long things changed. When this manager was later transferred to another organization, he became a most enthusiastic pro-
moter of the electrical wiring department. He understood its workings
and felt a part of it.

According to the Greeks enthusiasm means "God within us."
That's pretty strong stuff, but I guess that's why it gets action—and it

does. How do you get enthusiasm? Well, one way is by ensuring that the other person is thoroughly sold on the idea or action. Maybe he sees a way to get something he wants; maybe he has to do something to help develop the idea or maybe he participates in even a minor part of the action.

However your man comes to a task, get him involved so he has a stake in the outcome! Enthusiasm comes from within: that's where the action must also begin.

HOW TO MAKE IT EASY FOR HIM TO CHANGE HIS MIND TO YOUR WAY OF THINKING

While touring Italy last summer, Jane Rowe decided to purchase a piece of Venetian glass. She chose an expensive item and paid duty for it to be imported. When she got back to this country, the package arrived and to her horror she found the wrong bowl in it. Jane felt that she had been gypped and she was furious.

She sat down and wrote a letter that let the fire in her mind show. She then let the letter cool off for a day or two and decided to rewite it.

Jane began the letter: "While touring your enjoyable country last August, I had the pleasure of visiting Venice and your shop. There I purchased a . . ." and she went on to explain. Then she stated "It was an unavoidable error"—and later: "knowing you will want to do the right thing . . ." Toward the end, instead of saying, "You people will pay the expense of having the wrong item sent back and the new one sent over," she said, "I'm sure you will be willing to pay the expense of exchanging items."

Within a matter of weeks, she received a letter from Venice agreeing with everything she said: apologizing for the mistake and saying that the correct bowl would be rushed to her immediately. In addition, since the cost of return mailing was so great, they offered to let her buy the other bowl at half price. They were bending over backwards to make good their mistake.

That's how easy it is to let someone change his mind to your way of thinking. As managers, we may use the same technique.

One of Socrates' favorite methods of changing attitudes was through agreement. As he wandered around the streets of Athens where many people opposed his views, one of the ways he sold his opinions was by getting a man to agree on a familiar thought. Then he pursued another thought and got agreement, and gradually moved to the new area of thinking. The man was ready to agree because his mind had been led in a process of positive responses. Often a man can change his opinion if he is put in an agreeable mood. As a manager, part of your job is getting people to change their minds. Here are some tips to help you:

- Don't insult them personally.
- Don't infer that they would do wrong intentionally.
- Don't challenge what they say or do, so that they can't back up.
- Don't impugn their honor; in other words, leave them a way out or as the Orientals say, "Help them save face."

REFUSING ANYTHING LESS THAN RESULTS, NO MATTER HOW LOGICAL THE EXCUSE

If you've ever built a house, opened a store, extended a business, or had any construction work done, you can write this chapter yourself, provided you are still sane. Transfer a lesson from that experience to any dealing with people.

Several years ago, we built a new house. My wife was extremely proud of the fact that she was getting a slate floor in the entry hall. She was very particular about the color and the placement of the slate.

She was fighting mad when I came home one day. "Come out here and look at my entry hall," she said. Sure enough, the painters had painted the walls and dripped paint all over the slate. I told her to call them, tell them to come back and clean up the mess. She did.

However, when I came home again after they had finished the cleaning, she said, "Come and look." This time they had not really cleaned the slate; they merely smeared the paint and left. I told her to call once more and get them to try again.

On the third try the men managed to smear cleaning fluid around the edge of the wall and ruin the paint job. I told my wife to call them and get them to do the paint job over. They did it exactly! They slopped paint all over the slate floor again. Four tries later, the same situation existed because of sloppy service!

We didn't stop. We kept on until we got the floor cleaned. It is necessary to demand service in conjunction with getting action. The weak falter and pay dearly. We must learn to get what we pay for. We must learn to get it from people who work for us and from people who coordinate with us. Ask that any work or service be done over to your satisfaction even if it means doing it again and again.

STICK BY YOUR GUNS UNTIL YOU GET ACTION

Herb Jones told me that he's learned to stick by his guns.

Herb bought an Xmobile. At 24,000 miles the whole transmission fell apart: a line sprung a leak and the fluid drained out.

Herb called the car company. They said, "Sorry, but the warranty is only good for 24,000 miles. Talk to the corporation." The corporation said to talk to the dealer. The ball went back and forth.

After twelve calls, the corporation and dealer saw that Herb wasn't going to give up. Never did Herb raise his voice. His words were always challenging but, at the same time, always positive: "in the name of your reputation," etc. He knew he was right and that he wasn't going to pay even if he had to call a vice president in Detroit. Courteous determination paid off—and so did the auto company.

Herb's persistence won. If you're right, don't give up—don't give in. Don't stop short of complete satisfaction—but do it coolly and courteously. Above all, don't lose your temper unless you do it in a calculated manner.

Don't let the other fellow's run-around derail you. Refuse anything less than the results you want—stick by your guns.

Perhaps the name of this section out to be "persistence."

Remember the story of Warren and the real estate manager. Every other store owner had given up dealing with the manager because he was never in the office and never returned their calls when he came in. What did Warren do? At 1:45 P.M. he started calling person to person. The manager was on another phone; he left a number. At 2 P.M. there was no return call, Warren placed the person-to-person call again. Warren continued this every 15 minutes until 3:30 when he got through. The real estate manager realized that Warren was not to be turned off. An effective manager can't afford to be turned off if he's right and intends to get action—so stick to your guns.

HOW TO HANDLE THE KEY PERSON WHO WILL
GET RESULTS FROM THE TOP MAN

Is the controlling factor the boss's secretary? His administrative assistant? His staff man? Who has the key?

Steve Hale, sales manager of Ogilvie Produce needed to get in to talk with the manager of a large marketing association. Others had struck out here but Steve had to try his hand.

His first and most important step was to contact the receptionist and ask the secretary's name. Then he called her and said, "Alice, this is Steve Hale, with Ogilvie Produce. I'd like to talk with your manager about how we can help him. But I need some information. Can you tell me how many men he has working for him? and _____ and _____?"

Alice was pleased at his knowing her name. She was pleased at his knowing how important she was. She not only gave him the information but set up an appointment and helped him get what he wanted.

Defer to the influence of key persons and they'll throw their weight around on your side.

DETERMINING THE IMPORTANCE OF
PEOPLE-DEALING IN YOUR MANAGEMENT

There are two major approaches to getting the most from people: force and persuasion.

In applying force, we rely on a man doing a job because a person with authority tells him to. The key factor here is that his job is at stake: if he doesn't do something, he's fired. There is fear to consider in using force. The other approach is one of persuasion, or selling, which means appealing to an individual and causing him or her to want to do something.

One approach relies entirely on the flow of authority; the other, on motivation through personal selling, regardless of authority.

Let's consider the first approach. A young supervisor, Joe Doyle, had trouble with some of his employees. He called Sam into the office and discussed the difficulty. In no uncertain terms Joe told Sam that he would have to improve or else. Sam alternated between tears and anger, left the office—and improved. This is one case where a chewing-out worked. Why? Sam was obstinate, loud and brash. He had been warned before and was huffy. There are limited times when nothing beats an effective dressing-down and this was one of them. But any manager who relies on this as his standard approach is doomed to failure. Joe knew that Sam needed this particular kind of handling, yet if he handled everybody that way, he would be wrong. Joe must be able to vary his approach to suit the situation. Luckily, he can. Try both of these approaches to people-dealing and arrive at your own best technique. But begin by assuring yourself that a knowledge of handling people effectively will be your key to getting action.

Note what turned up in one large industry:

An executive development session was attended by all of the managers of a major organization. During the session, these men had to rate each other on many of their qualities. They were men who were not just casually associated: most of them had worked with each other for 10 to 15 years and knew each other thoroughly.

Two men ranked high in people-dealing, but lowest in technical knowledge. Two other men came out very high in technical knowledge and very low in people-dealing. Within six months, the two who were high in people-dealing had moved up one notch in their jobs. The two who were rock bottom in that quality had moved down a peg; in fact, one finally left the company. In this experience, people-dealing was the top priority skill.

Really sell yourself on the importance of knowing how to handle people. It's far easier to do technical work and to hire people with technical ability than it is to find a man adroit in managing people. Make it a top priority for your men.

SUCCESSFUL WAYS TO DEAL UP THE LINE

In the executive development session mentioned earlier, another experiment was tried. Each manager was asked to handle three human relations situations. Each situation called for correction of a fault in another individual—without having the other explode. In one case, the subject assumed he was dealing with somebody working directly *below him*. In the next case, he would be dealing with somebody across the line on an *equal level*, but not in his own organization. In the third case, he was asked to talk with *his boss* about correcting a fault. It was found that in correcting someone down the line, the supervisor found it very easy to be blunt and completely honest, and to discount any of the desires of the individual. The second situation found the man using a little more tact and salesmanship as he talked to someone across the line. He gave more consideration and was a little more cautious; he considered the other individual. In the third situation, when he was talking up the line, he began pussyfooting. He not only was soft-spoken but used every human relations rule he knew. When he realized he had built-in authority, one thing happened. When he realized that he was going upstream, another; and across the line, yet another. If the manager handling the situation were really concerned with the other individual as a human being and not as a tool in his hands, then he would consider every man the same. It is pretty hard to persuade a manager to do this. I'm not saying everyone should be handled the same, but that we should be aware that we change our direction because of rank or authority and not because of individual personality needs.

Here are some ideas:

- If the atmosphere is such that a man likes to be called by his first name, call him by his first name the first time you meet him—then do it every time you see him.
- Always defer to rank. But don't kowtow to it. People love to be treated like human beings.
- Be considerate of your prospect's time and get on with your work and out of his way. If you have a long session, feel him out along the line to see if you're imposing.
- Above all else, act with confidence in dealing with him; that's what he's paying you for.

HOW TO USE FUNCTIONAL AUTHORITY AND GET ACTION ACROSS THE LINE

A small manufacturing plant employing about 500 people had a high degree of interpersonal and functional interface between various functions and levels of management. All members of management appeared to be dedicated to doing a good job. The plant still had growing pains from expansion last year (both in operator effectiveness and management systems) and these two areas of concern reflected themselves in costs, schedule, and quality. Supervision seemed at times to work around the system rather than through it—a combination of not knowing the system itself and not knowing how to make the system work. The management group was eager to strengthen its management team effectiveness for the attainment of organizational goals. The management team wanted to tighten up its management controls, particularly in the fabrication, use and accountability of tools and fixtures.

The managers were asked by their president to define the reasons they didn't get results. They cited poor communications, lack of clear-cut goals, lack of follow-up on corrective actions, failure to create interest and desire for excellence among personnel, insufficient team work, lack of order and organization, insufficient interest and support from other organizations, and failure to delegate responsibility. It was a hotbed where functional authority needed to be operating at its best.

Into this mess stepped Herm Neal. As head of manufacturing engineering, he drew up a plan for controlling work flow, supplies and parts. Instead of selling it, he tried to force it. He left in a heat!

John Cowart succeeded with almost the same plan, but he

a. Got to know each affected individual.

b. Showed an eager interest in them.

c. Explained simply the needed changes and interface from department to department.

d. Praised the slightest improvement any individual or department made.

e. Gave others credit for the changes.

He knew how to sell himself and how to praise, so he came through a winner. The employees thought he was great and management got their changes.

If you're going across lines, take time to sell your plan and gain acceptance. Even if it's a little slower, it is the only force you have and can be enough to do a functional job.

KEEPING THE LINE OPEN FOR INCOMING
MESSAGES THAT CAN INFLUENCE
YOUR DIRECTION

Your drive for action must be strong, but if you close communications in the process then you may miss your target.

Joe May got a call from one of his men in the data collection center of a shipping company. Joe, fortunately, is a smart enough manager to help get his man out of a jam. Joe's man, Bill, stated, "Come out here and let me show you where the system doesn't work." When he arrived, it was easy for Joe to see that his assistant and the clerk were furious.

Bill said, "They won't take this form and process it." The clerk stated, "We are not supposed to take it. It's supposed to be on an XYZ form." Bill then pulled out a procedure that seemed to support him.

"Let's go to the office and study it," suggested Joe and told the clerk not to worry about it and they'd let him know later.

Sure enough, the clerk was right. When they went back and told him so, he beamed as if to say "I told you so." But then he immediately went to work helping get the right form and the report submitted. He couldn't do enough for them.

But a few more minutes with Bill earlier would have closed the door forever. Joe knows how to keep communication going with an individual even though the exchange is hot. You might need a man to finalize the action, so keep the lines open.

Perhaps the most important points made in this chapter are:

1. Put people-dealing first on your list of management skills.

2. Try several ways to arrive at your own best style.

3. Stick by your guns until you get results.

4. Keep your relationship on a good enough basis for results this time and in the future.

How to Get
The Results You Want
with Every Letter
You Write*

12

"One of the greatest deficiencies we find in employees today is the lack of ability to express themselves well in writing. In fact, many of them shy away from doing it if they can find another way."

Such were the words of William F. James, Chief, Employee Development and Incentives Division of a large Department of Defense field activity, as he addressed a joint Government/Industry personnel training panel.

He further stated, "This should not be the case. If we could find a *magic formula* for converting that deficiency into an adequate, common, everyday skill, such as walking, talking, or driving a car, we could easily increase our efficiency 25-30% or perhaps even more!"

Just as surely as there are recipes for a delicate French cuisine, there is a magic formula for effective business writing. In fact, it applies to all forms of communication, either oral or written, and it's not hard to use or understand.

The formula can be stated in a very few words and just as easily remembered. If you would like to be able to write more successfully, quickly, and surely, simply be a *Speed Mason*!

"Hold everything!" you say. "I know what a brick mason is, or even a stone mason, but what's a *Speed Mason*?"

---

*William M. Parr, *Executive's Guide to Effective Letters and Reports* (West Nyack, N.Y.: Parker Publishing Company, Inc., 1976).

Obviously, a little explanation is in order here. Let's consider at first the definitions. A mason is "a skilled workman who builds with stone or similar material." Speed is defined as "the act or state of moving quickly, or to further the success of something." We can therefore state that a SPEED MASON is a person who builds, rather quickly and successfully, with strong material on a firm foundation to achieve a specific objective.

The objective in this case is to be able to write more successfully, in a reasonably rapid fashion, to our customers and business associates. I'm sure many people you know have made the observation that one of their biggest problems was lack of communication.

One of the biggest obstacles to good communication is not in what has been said, but in what has *not* been said. A learned authority once made the observation, "You must write not so that you can be understood, but so that you *cannot possibly be misunderstood*."

It's an old truism: If you want to overcome or resolve a problem, first you have to *identify* the problem, and then take appropriate steps to correct it. This may well be true, but we have to reckon with a basic failure of human nature. Even though a person knows a problem exists, he either cannot or does not want to recognize the nature of it.

Many well-educated people will not admit they are not good writers. As with many other things, the resolution of the problem has to start with the individual.

Possibly the biggest hurdle to overcome in the pursuit of truly effective communication is the wrong mental attitude of the writer. It is safe to say the great majority of people do not know what good letter writing requires.

Many well-informed executives will say, when asked, that good letter writing requires reasonably correct grammar and spelling as well as a good command of the English language. These are certainly necessary, but they are not the most important. More than anything else, good letter writing requires applied psychology or skill in the art of human relations. Second, it needs to use the *language that motivates*.

Success of any plan, mission, or idea can usually result only from effective communication. Good communication can result only from an *aroused* individual with an intense *desire* to create a better channel of understanding so he can *transfer* his belief to another person.

In addition to the definitions of the words as just described, SPEED MASON is an acronym I have designed to represent and help you remember the ten most essential "*how*" elements used to achieve successful communication. Without most of them, successful communication is impossible and, without successful communication, effective writing is also impossible. They are:

Soul	Motivation
Planning and Preparation	Acceptability
Emotional Stability	Simplicity
Evaluation	Organization
Direction	Novelty

Instead of trying to recall what ten items are essential to good writing and becoming confused, think of the term "SPEED MASON" and the elements will automatically spring into your consciousness. Not only will you be better prepared, but you will have a stronger feeling of self-confidence by knowing you can remember and use them at will.

Put them all into use and you will, in almost every case, write well. At least, if you establish good communication, one of your biggest problems will have been resolved.

Admittedly, knowledge alone does not always insure achievement. Even knowledge, application, and hard work does not always produce results. Only if we know *how* or *why* something is done can we be reasonably sure of success.

The phrase "Be a *Speed Mason!*" is one short way of combining several factual elements into an easy-to-remember form and, by remembering it, we can put them to *use* more often and more effectively. Each facet of communication, be it oral or written, must recognize and properly utilize each of these elements.

Let's consider carefully the meaning behind each one:

SOUL

Most people will agree today that soul is important in the social and personal sense, even in the political sense, but they are not too quick to admit it has an important place in the truly business sense. I challenge that!

Maybe it is a cruel business world we live in. Maybe we should not expect the proper amount of consideration in our dealings with our business associates, but conditions are changing. Businessmen who have not been aware of or responsive to feelings and reactions of those with whom they have tried to communicate have long since paid the price.

A young securities salesman I know wrote a letter recently to a prospective client asking for an appointment. Two weeks passed without a reply from the gentleman, who owned a chain store. Then one day they met at a businessman's lunch. When they were introduced the chain store man said, "I hope you'll forgive me for not answering your letter. I'll be glad to have you come around and see me any time."

"Fine," said the securities man, pleased at the friendly invitation, "I wondered why you didn't answer."

"If you want to know the truth." the chain store owner explained, "your letter gave me the idea that you were pretty much of a stuffed shirt. Now that we've met, I realize you're a nice guy I'd be happy to talk to."

This young man discovered something that many people have learned in recent years—the letters we write can give a false picture of us. They can make us appear selfish instead of generous, pompous rather than personable, flippant when we mean to be friendly. For the recipients, the picture our letters paint is our personality, for better or worse. With care we can make our letters reveal the more attractive rather than the worse side of our nature.

Soul is the term used here because of what it is: the embracing of all understanding, human feeling, empathy, consideration for the needs and desires of other people. In many ways, we see only through our own eyes, or in a strictly subjective sense. It is the ordinary thing to do, the human thing, the easy way. A twentieth century philosopher has submitted that the major elements of SOUL are indicated by the letters of the word itself:

S incerity
O pen-mindedness
U nderstanding
L ove

There's nothing wrong with that. Do we have to be less tolerant, less patient, less understanding to prove we are better people? That strikes me as an anomaly. It seems pretty obvious that if we try to practice these elements in our daily lives, we would encourage others to do the same thing. The obvious result would be better communication.

Being human in the real sense (looking at a subject from the *reader's* point of view) creates a vehicle for better communication and will go a long way toward attaining our objectives. Taking heed of a person's problems, analyzing them, and giving the writer or reader the impression he is important to us brings about many benefits which create greater harmony, develop cooperation, and enable us to be much more effective.

In addition to developing greater understanding, it inspires confidence and trust, earns respect and generates more harmonious relationships. Moreover, it makes the reader feel important, encourages friendships, and produces more team work. Finally, and more important, it also helps to sell your ideas.

What are some of the tricks that words can play on us if we are not careful? Here's an example from a letter received the other day by a neighbor of mine who had asked two contractors for bids on a concrete driveway. One letter went like this:

> Dear Mr. Dawson:
> I am offering you a special price on this job because I am having a slack season just now, and my partner and I like to keep busy. I have some debts to pay and this work will be a big help to me. I would appreciate your patronage.

The first paragraph showed that the writer was suffering from a bad case of "I-me-itis." Not only the constant use of "I," "my," and "me," but the whole tone of the letter reveals the writer was thinking of *himself*, not of the person he was writing to. My neighbor's reaction was, "He sounds like a selfish kind of guy."

This man had violated the first rule of good letter writing: *Take the* You *attitude.* In other words, think of your reader's problems and forget about your own if you want to interest him.

The second contractor wrote as follows:

> Dear Mr. Dawson:
> I can give you a good, solid driveway with a 6-inch bed of cinders and 3 inches of concrete. Properly graded and drained, this could last you 10 to 20 years without cracking.

This man got the job because he told the customer what he wanted to know—what he would get, what he would be served, and what good it would do him—not how much good it would do the contractor to get the work.

It is surprising how many letters disclose, unknown to the writer, a suspicious, distrustful, antagonistic attitude toward the person to whom the letter is addressed. Somehow things we would never say to an individual face to face often creep into our correspondence.

So an all-important rule to follow is *Practice Courtesy!*

This means generous use in correspondence of "please," "thank you," "I'm glad," "I appreciate," etc. Words which rub the reader the wrong way—"We suspect," "You misunderstood," or "We can hardly believe"—are eliminated from the persuasive letter writer's vocabulary.

After these rules of letter writing have been mastered, there is still an undefinable quality or tone in a letter which comes from the personality of the writer. It can't be taught, but it can be learned. Maybe the following will show what I mean. It was written by the recently elected president of a large company to an associate of mine:

> Dear Ed:
> You are a generous and thoughtful friend as always to take the trouble to write me about my new job.
> I deeply appreciate your good wishes, to which I hope you may add a prayer or two. There are bound to be some occasions when I will need both.
> My thanks and only the best.
> Sincerely,
> Bill

Notice for one thing, this letter is extremely informal. In the business and professional world today, dry, impersonal salutations, such as "Dear Sir" are rarely used. In writing to a stranger or someone we don't know well, we use the man's name, "Dear Mr. Randolph." Among personal or business friends, the first name or a nickname appears on most letters nowadays—the same name we'd use if we met the man on the street.

If you want to look at the other side of the coin, appreciating and understanding the other person's point of view counteracts, to a large degree, feelings of fear, hate, distrust, selfishness, greed, envy, jealousy, impatience, the urge to "get even," misinterpretations, indifference, and lack of motivation. My question is: Why run the risk?

PLANNING AND PREPARATION

If you can go into battle without being prepared and without fear, you must surely have been born with .45 caliber revolvers for hands. To do otherwise is pure folly. Why then do so many of us try to sell an idea or a product, get people to take action, or put across our point of view, without being properly prepared?

If we don't sell our idea or succeed in our efforts to win converts for what we want to do, then who can we really blame but ourselves? As they say: "We haven't done our homework."

Preparation, in the truest sense, covers several things—that is, preparation not only of the subject matter involved, but also of the *individual* we are addressing, as well as devising the proper *approach* to gain acceptance.

It is almost axiomatic that nothing fruitful or beneficial will occur unless you plan things out so that it will take place. More than likely, anything beneficial that results without a plan is purely accidental.

This is a good time to bring up a problem or, should I say, the resolution of a problem that many people, principally supervisors, are faced with. The sad part of it is that they don't realize they have a problem. That problem, simply stated, is dictating a letter or a short report to a stenographer.

Much valuable time and effort is lost, in both Government and industry, because an individual does not dictate—preferring instead to write a letter out in longhand. The writer may think it will be more accurate, concise, and complete if it is written out, but is it worth all the effort and, more important, is it really all that difficult to dictate to someone?

Many people have confided to me, "I never realized how easy it was until I got the hang of it." Don't put yourself down. Don't say to yourself, "It's too much trouble," or "It's easier for me to write it out." Give yourself a chance. Try it once.

Another fact you may have overlooked is that your secretary is *supposed* to take shorthand. She would like to keep her "hand in," as it were. So you would be doing both of you a favor if you decided to give it a whirl.

Statistics show the average one page letter takes 42 minutes to develop, compose, and write in longhand. Assuming it took 10 to 12 minutes to get your material ready for dictation, it would take only two or three minutes to dictate. The whole letter would take less than half as long, and you would not have to write anything at all except, of course, some basic notes. Even if your secretary typed out your dictated notes in rough draft, you shouldn't have to spend more than two or three more minutes to edit. Then she could type final copy. Look at the time you would save!

The secret to being able to dictate effectively is merely being prepared for it. *You have to be prepared* to write, even though you do write it out yourself. So why not give your secretary a chance to help?

EMOTIONAL STABILITY

A veritable "bee in the bonnet," this element causes the most trouble and is the hardest to control. Many things are forever lost because we let an emotion, or maybe several of them, get in our way or take over our reason. This is more true of relationships with relatives than with business associates, of course, but it is still just as damaging to our interests.

Emotion can have infinite variety. It isn't just anger, hate, or envy. It can be greed, bias, prejudice, passion, infatuation, jealousy, false pride—any number of things. Emotion in its place (except where it destroys) is a desirable thing, but it will always cloud the way to clear thinking. The most unfortunate thing is in the fact that a great many people are guilty of having their decisions and their communications clouded by an emotion, or several of them.

This element is just as important on the other side (the reader) as it is to the writer. If the reader is angry, frustrated, or grief-stricken, the writer has a difficult task in trying to communicate with him. The reader's reasoning process is clouded with emotion. It would often pay dividends if you tried to determine whether your reader will be in the proper frame of mind when he gets your letter.

Let's suppose for a moment a Mr. Al Johnson had opened a charge account at your store several years ago and had been paying his bills on a timely basis until recently when, for some unknown reason, he stopped making payments.

You found out he owed $256.00 and had made no payments for the past three months. The bookkeeper has sent him a past due notice the first month and a form letter the second month with no results. You decided to "take the bull by the horns" and write him the following letter:

Dear Mr. Johnson:
Our records indicate that you have owed us $256. for well over three months. We have written you about this matter several times before, but you failed to reply.
As explained to you when you opened your account, credit is extended only to customers who agree to repay their bills on a regular basis.
Therefore, we must ask for immediate payment of this bill in full. If you do not reply to this letter within 15 days, we will be forced to turn your account over to our attorney for appropriate action.
Very truly yours,
A.B. Samuels

What would you say the odds are on your getting payment of the overdue bill of $256.00? I would say your chances are (1) very small or (2) none at all.

You have undoubtedly satisfied your own exasperation over the apparent advantage a good customer has taken of you. But have you really accomplished anything? Have you considered any other possibilities, such as:

- Mr. Johnson is out of town?
- There may be illness or a death in the family?
- Mr. Johnson has suffered severe financial reverses and is ashamed to tell you about them?
- The customer has a complaint against the store and you are actually at fault?
- His payment was made but has been lost or misplaced?
- He has moved and his mail is not reaching him?

There are other ways to handle this particular problem, but the solution does not lie in issuing an ultimatum—at least, not before all other alternatives have been exhausted.

If you stop to think about it, emotional stability accomplishes quite a lot. It quiets an upset mind, inspires confidence, clears thought processes, and generally lowers blood pressure. You can help bring it about by being courteous, honest, tactful, patient, and thinking ahead to possible reactions to how you are going to express something.

An extremely hard person to communicate with is a person who has decided he is right and, when challenged, immediately adopts a "how dare you question my opinion?" attitude. Don't laugh—you might be guilty of this too.

A person who cannot admit he is wrong soon becomes a buckpasser. The two things go together. Someone else has to be responsible. Being wrong is certainly neither a disgrace nor a disaster, but refusing to admit that you are wrong can become one.

EVALUATION

Writing for a purpose without looking it over once in a while to see if it is going to do what you want, or has already done so, is like a chef cooking a dinner without testing it. It would be a huge gamble indeed to sit back and hope for the best.

Many people go about the business of trying to communicate with others every day and never realize that they might not be doing it properly or perhaps could do it better. They would probably say, "It's too much trouble to worry about it."

One good way to evaluate how well you are writing something is to try it out on a friend and to be *alert* to reactions on his part. He will show in many ways whether he is getting your message, or is even interested in it. If you are aware of these signs, you can and should make some changes.

One thing that should always be expected is the unexpected. No one can ever exactly anticipate what reception an idea will get. The reaction might even bring about improvements on the original idea that you did not anticipate.

A frequent cause of lack of acceptance of an idea is not understanding the *language* used. One should always evaluate carefully whether the terminology being used is in the proper jargon or level of understanding of the listener or reader.

Anyone using a written form of communication can never be satisfied that it will always produce the desired results. Whether it is a direct mail campaign, procedural instructions, or group training, the results must be tested, measured, and revised to fit the needs of the moment. Only in this way can we be sure our message is going to get across the way we want it to and bring about satisfactory achievement of our objective. Nowhere is the old adage more appropriate: "Haste makes waste!"

I recently saw a memorandum from an executive in a large company which read, "If John Martin will see Jim Abbott and get the details, I'll talk to him later." Who was to be talked to in this case remained a mystery!

Examples like this lead us to another highly important rule in letter writing: *Say clearly what you mean!* When this rule is broken, it's often the result of hurrying. Before starting to write a letter, it is a good idea to think through what you want to say and the best way of saying it.

As added insurance, every letter you send out should be read over carefully before the envelope is sealed. When we use words that are confusing, in the wrong place, or with the wrong meaning, this tells the reader that we are careless and muddleheaded—qualities which inspire doubt rather than confidence.

DIRECTION

If a super businessman could analyze every failure of the past fifty years, chances are he would find most of them were caused by lack of direction. According to E. Joseph Cossman, Mail-Order Millionaire, 92% of all business failures are due to lack of direction; direction at the top; direction down the line; direction whenever a crossroads is reached or a decision has to be made.

The *proper* direction at every turn will go far in assuring the success of any venture. This is equally as important in communication, for communication without direction is like an automobile running down the street without a driver. Everyone wants direction.

Look for a moment into your past. You have seen many an occasion when a little direction given by the proper party could have avoided a loss of prestige, a loss of business, or even a tragic consequence.

A simple example of lack of direction is seen in the following instruction:

"When the authorization form is received and validated with the Treasurer's letter, it will be forwarded to the Finance Unit."

What is to be forwarded—the form, the letter, or both?

Direction is important to everyone. It points the way, it helps someone to decide, it brings organization out of chaos, it shows priorities, it highlights important points, it identifies objectives and arranges them in logical order. It helps your reader to follow you down the path to the conclusion you want him to reach.

You would readily admit you can't follow an overall strategy, approach, or procedure unless someone has designed a plan and told you how to follow it through. Putting the shoe on the other foot, how could you expect someone to do what you want him to, unless you show him how or give him a clear written instruction to follow?

MOTIVATION

Motivation, not love, is what makes the world go 'round! If we are able, by whatever means we can employ, to incite someone to act in our behalf, we have succeeded in *motivating* him. If we have not or cannot do it, for whatever reason, we have failed to motivate and, if we have failed to motivate, we have *failed* in our objective.

Many people still ask the question, "What really is motivation?" Reams of material and thousands of words have been written on the subject. The basic and perhaps best definition is the dictionary version, which says that motivation is "something that causes a person to act; an incentive, inducement, or a stimulus to action." Isn't this after all, what we are trying to do when we communicate with others?

Motivation is not really a big word when we understand how it works. Boiled down to its barest essentials, *motivation* and *emotion* go hand in hand like ham and eggs, or shoes and socks.

Emotion is created by *verbal, live and active words, descriptive and sympathetic terms, or simple and exciting verbs.* So, too, is motivation to act. If you would stimulate anyone to action, look to your language. If it is dull and stodgy, devoid of action and, in most cases, long and drawn out, you will have trouble motivating even your best friend.

There are two ways to look at every situation—call them positive and negative, downbeat and upbeat, or simply gloomy and cheerful.

Many writers reveal unwittingly their fears and doubts rather than the constructive ideas they want.

This leads up to another extremely important rule for good letter writing: *Accentuate the positive!*

For example, a large manufacturer of building materials found not long ago that a new type of asbestos shingle was not selling as well as an older style, although it was superior. A young man handling orders for the company wrote the following letter:

> Dear Mr. Paine:
> I am sorry to tell you that we no longer make the kind of shingles you inquired about. We have, however, a new style which may fit your needs.

This apologetic, negative approach was changed around by inverting the order of statements as well as the tone:

> Dear Mr. Paine:
> I am happy to send you samples of our new roofing shingle, which now comes in a wider range of colors and textures than before. It is a great improvement on the old style, which it has replaced.

Both letters told the truth, but the second one took a positive approach which made the reader *want to see* the new shingles, instead of making him *sorry* about the discontinuance of the old style. Sales in the department began to rise almost immediately.

Before leaving this subject, we perhaps should give you a fairly modern, time-tested technique for using Motivation to get your reader to respond the way you want him to. You might say it is actually four techniques in one:

1. *Put the reader in the picture* with proper use of the **You** attitude. To capture his interest and understanding, you must first capture his attention. What better way to do it than to talk about *his* interests?

2. *Appeal to the reader's emotion.* As stated earlier, people respond first with the heart, then with the mind. This, of course, requires a continuation of the **You** attitude.

3. *Convince the reader's mind.* Now that you have successfully

insured your reader's attention, you can bring into play your facts and logic. Only now you can safely begin to use "we."

4. *Stimulate your reader to action*, still with a continuation of the "we" attitude. Show him **Why** it will pay to act *now*. Ask for the order, or show him why he will either gain by acting right away, or lose something of value if he fails to act.

If you practice this technique as you should, I can practically guarantee results.

ACCEPTABILITY

Communication frequently breaks down for one principal reason: Mental Rejection. For many psychological reasons, people resist the input of new ideas into their storehouse of knowledge. Primarily, it interferes with their normal routines or their established way of doing things.

The word *acceptable* covers many things. First of all, it includes or implies anything which is rational, fair or logical. Many times an idea is rejected because it does not meet this test, and the writer does not realize he has not made his point.

Until the writer puts together an idea or a concept which can be accepted, he is wasting his time covering the other points. In other words, he is not communicating with the reader.

Another facet of acceptability is that of "speaking the same language" as the reader. If the author is not using words, terminology, or jargon with which the reader is familiar, the latter will *reject* it because he doesn't understand it.

He may not perhaps realize he doesn't understand, or he may simply be afraid to show his ignorance and ask for clarification. He will just wait for something to come along he can accept. The fact that the writer has not in fact reached the reader may never come to light.

One of the biggest problems a writer will face is *misinterpretation*—that of assuming a meaning not intended. Rather than being acceptability in the strictest sense, we might call it a fault created by *over-acceptability*. The reader is always in a hurry to get the message, or accept the idea being expressed, especially if it agrees with his own. Thus, he frequently falls into the trap of getting the *wrong* message or idea completely.

Hundreds of words, perhaps even thousands, have *double* meanings. It is one of the pitfalls of the English language. The word "priceless" is one example. Does it mean "without price" and therefore cheap, or does it mean so high in value that money couldn't buy it?

More significant and perhaps a much greater problem than the double-meaning word is the use of a word *out of context*. This occurs when we use a word from our frame of reference, but it doesn't have the same meaning from someone else's frame of reference—words like rich, poor, hot, cold, dumb, smart, short, tall, old, new, etc.

For example, if a native of Arizona was to describe the weather of a certain location as cold, a native of Montana would probably scoff and say, "Why, that's shirt-sleeve weather in my home town!"

One of the best ways to avoid this problem in trying to get your message across is to put yourself in your reader's shoes, or *think in his terms*. In other words, ask yourself, "What is his background, his level of understanding, what impression is he likely to get from what I say?"

If you give the proper amount of thought to this principle as often as you can *before* you write on a subject, you will go a long way in preventing a communication breakdown.

Still another measure of acceptability is whether something is *important* or *beneficial* to the reader. This is a continual process of evaluation on his part for, when he reaches a point in time of deciding that it is neither, he will "turn you off" mentally. This is why it is so important to make as favorable an impression as you can on your reader *before* you get down to the main issues.

One final thought on the subject. A strange thing occurs when a thought, being transmitted in writing, is not *completely or properly expressed*. The mind of the reader says, "Whoops! That idea does not make sense at all; therefore, I will reject it completely!"

This is the reason people who have trouble either constructing or finishing a sentence also have a lot of trouble communicating. This problem more often than not creates an inferiority complex and makes these people less willing to communicate. This tends, of course, to compound the problem even further.

SIMPLICITY

Whatever happened to the simple life? Why is life so complicated? Is it because we consider it the fashionable thing to do? Are we afraid to say we don't really understand the complex and be thought uneducated, unsophisticated, or even inferior?

One of the hardest lessons for the average writer to learn is that everyone he writes to is not on the same level of understanding of the subject as he is. This is not to imply that the writer is superior or that the reader is inferior, but the writer has had to become well versed on the subject, else he could not transfer that knowledge to others.

This is another area where mental rejection plays a highly significant part. The mind of the reader says, "It's too complicated; I don't understand it; I won't accept it."

You obviously wouldn't preach physical theorems to a music student, even though the latter might have a high I.Q. The sad part of it is, if you do, your message has gone "over the head" of the reader, and there is no easy way to make you aware of it.

This brings us to another highly important guide to more effective letter writing: *Be Yourself!* The best letters are written as you would talk, in everyday language.

A recent Government pamphlet campaigns for the same thing, which it labels "straightaway English." The authors point out that official jargon or "gobbledygook" wastes time, tax money, and storage space. The booklet recommends that long, stuffed-shirt expressions, such as "ameliorate," "compliance," and "enclosed please find" should be tossed in the wastebasket, and suggests bureaucratic letter writers stick to the simple things, like brevity and sincerity.

The businessman who uses such phrases as, "Yours of the 7th," "Agreeable to your communication," and "Receipt is acknowledged of . . ." gives the impression he is a pompous egotist who has no friendly feeling for the person he's writing to. If you want to tell someone you received his letter, why not say, "I received your letter letter and . . ."?

Another rule for good letter writing which closely parallels the previous one is: *Be thrifty with words!*

The other day I saw a letter which began like this: "Mr. Long has offered a suggestion regarding a departure from our standard procedure with respect to remuneration for overtime employment." I don't go any farther, because I had to stop and figure out what all those words meant. If the writer had simply said, "Mr. Long suggested a new way to pay for overtime," I'd have been interested at once!

Simplicity (and that includes brevity, clarity, and conciseness) greatly enhances mental understanding, acceptance of an idea, maintains the reader's interest, makes objectives more plain and easier to achieve, and generally improves the learning situation.

The use of cartoons, diagrams, and photographs has proven many times the advantage of making things simple.

ORGANIZATION

Strange as it may seem, many people do things well, but they never seem to get organized. One would think none of the other elements mentioned above could be very effective at all if what you write is not properly organized.

The reason this element is so important to good communication and is specifically mentioned is the fact that the majority of people speak without thinking or sit down and write without getting all the necessary information together and arranging it in logical sequence.

Webster's Collegiate Dictionary defines the word *organize* as: "To arrange or form into a coherent unity or functioning whole . . . to arrange elements into a whole of interdependent parts."

To make any letter, report, procedure, or simple instruction have the effect you need or desire, it must be properly organized for the maximum impact, e.g., the "attention-getter" right on top, the next most important points near the top, etc. All the necessary items must be included, the unnecessary and extraneous must be excluded, and what is used should be arranged to present your material in its most forceful light.

Much good material is often wasted in a long letter or a report simply because it was poorly or inefficiently organized. So, if you want to put your best foot forward, look to your organization!

NOVELTY

Why is this element so important? You ask, "Will it help me write a better letter?" It has been proven many times that the *most satisfactory* communication experience resulted from a *novel or different approach*. The reason for this is because the author *attracted attention* with it.

Most everyone knows the first and foremost action in getting a speaker's point across is to get the listener's attention. If he is successful, the speaker can proceed with reasonable assurance that his next point will at least be heard, whether it is understood or not.

If he is not successful, he might as well pack up and go home, for now he has nowhere else to go with his message. This is even more important in writing, because it is harder to hold someone's attention with the written word. For example:

> Dear Mr. Chalmers:
> We have just heard from Mr. Fran Ellison, who calls on you, about your wife's recent operation. We were indeed sorry . . .

Wouldn't you agree that Mr. Chalmers is going to take the time to read that letter? You bet he is! First of all, it shows effective use of the "You attitude."

In addition, Mr. Chalmers is undoubtedly interested in what you might say about his wife. Your concern also shows you to be the type of individual he can trust—or at least, it so appears. This is mainly because your interest in the reader is greater than your interest in yourself.

The novel approach doesn't have to be exciting, funny or dramatic to be different, but it should cause some *favorable reaction* on the part of the reader. Sometimes this approach can be equally effective by not being dramatic. Anything that amuses, shocks, makes an impression, or otherwise gains attention may be considered a successful opening.

The best way, perhaps, to find a novel beginning is to ask yourself, "What can I offer that is different?" You will be surprised, oftentimes pleased, at what you come up with.

In summary, the ten elements we have outlined tie together to form adequate communication, and that means improved writing skill. None of these elements, good as they are, have any substance or meaning, unless they are properly conveyed to the reader.

Whether writing a simple letter or a report, or detailing complex procedures, you will be successful only to the degree that you give adequate consideration to these factors. If you consciously apply this Magic Formula, you will find it truly puts POWER into your writing.

How to Win with Words that Everybody Knows, Uses, and Understands*

13

In some ways this might be called the Age of Writing. Nearly everyone is called upon to write something every day. The boss sends instructions to his salesmen, employees report on the day's activities in writing, the housewife jots notes to her children, and students write papers on every conceivable subject.

Yet, bad writing causes an almost incalculable amount of damage and trouble. Good writing, on the other hand, can pay off handsomely.

For instance, Ralph Miller, a factory foreman who couldn't understand the complex written rules and regulations on his income tax form, saved almost $500 by following six concise, written rules given him by a local C.P.A.

Bill White, a Spokane, Washington bus driver, saved $400 by following precise written instructions on how to take the family at half-rate to a well-known resort.

Sam Grimes, a small machinery manufacturing company salesman, made the company $1000 because he communicated concisely in a written memo exactly how to receive an extra bonus by shipping immediately. And George Hendricks, a shipping clerk, received a

---

*Duane Newcomb, *Word Power Makes the Difference: Making What You Write Pay Off* (Englewood Cliffs, N.J.: Prentice-Hall, Inc., 1975).

special $300 reward from his company for the excellent written communication that his two-man office turned out.

Actually clear, concise, easy-to-understand writing offers many advantages. The problem is that the more difficult you make a piece of writing, the less your reader will understand it. At first, he'll simply miss some of the points you're trying to make, but, finally, if you make it difficult enough he'll stop reading altogether.

Ever wonder why, for instance, you couldn't learn easily from a textbook? Chances are it wasn't because the subject was difficult, but because the author didn't explain the subject matter clearly. Recent tests have shown that students actually learn three or four times faster than they normally would when the text material is uncomplicated.

There are other benefits from clear, concise communications: mistakes decrease, readers can read the written material faster and retain more, and everyday life in general becomes simpler. As a result, plain talk actually has the power to save every one of us time, money, and energy in almost every activity that involves the written word.

Learning to communicate clearly only accounts for one third of the word power tools that will make your writing produce action. Yet it is extremely important, for unless you can communicate clearly you will never be able to use the other word power tools effectively. In this chapter you will take up the Plain Talk side of clear communication, learning how to keep sentence length in check, how to come to the point immediately, how to write as you talk, and how to get rid of unnecessary words that diffuse meaning.

CHECK IT WITH A READABILITY INDEX

Just how do you know when you're writing plainly? You don't, not unless you have a guide, and there are some good ones available. But before I give you a readability guide to use in your own writing let's consider what people prefer to read.

Probably the most universally read magazine in the United States today is the *Reader's Digest*. Millions "devour" it every month and almost everyone can understand it easily. *Sports Illustrated, McCalls* and *Newsweek* are also read by an extremely large audience. They are a little more difficult to read than *Reader's Digest*, but certainly clear and understandable. As we move toward the *Atlantic Monthly* and *Harper's Magazine* we begin to lose our audience. These last two are considered primarily "highbrow" magazines and almost all of their readers are both college-trained and intellectually inclined. Beyond this, we find technical writing, government information (but not all), textbooks, and similar material which very few readers will even try to read unless it's absolutely necessary.

Obviously then, to get through to your readers effectively, you should stay somewhere in the middle range of the *Reader's Digest, Sports Illustrated, McCalls, Newsweek,* and similar magazines. The question is, of course, just what is this middle range? There are a number of readability guides. The one developed by Rudolf Flesch, and Robert Gunning's *Fog Count* are probably two of the best, but I find both a little cumbersome to use, so I will outline one here which can be applied a little more easily to your writing.

(1) Count the number of sentences in a sample of 100 words and divide the number of sentences into 100. (This is the average number of words per sentence.) (2) Count all the words over seven letters in length. (3) Add both figures together and divide the sum by two. This gives you a workable readability index. For instance, a 100 word passage with six sentences and six words with over seven letters each adds up this way: 100/6 equals 16. 16 plus 6 equals 22. Divide this by 2, and you have a readability index of 11.

Here's how some well-known reading material tests out:

Children's writing	10–12
General magazines	13–15
Literary magazines	17–20
Most textbooks, technical materials	23 plus

For good readability then you should try to keep your own writing within a readability index of 12 to 16. Several studies have shown that employees that communicate best are those who get the better jobs and are promoted fastest. In addition, people who keep their writing in this range get more action, better understanding from others, and an overall favorable response.

KEEP SENTENCE LENGTH IN CHECK

People read in sentences, not in words. Research over the last 20 years to determine the effect of sentence length on readability has shown that the longer a sentence is, the harder it is to read.

Here is a gauge:

Very Easy	8 words or less per sentence
Easy	9–11 words
Fairly Easy	12–14 words
Average	15–19 words
Fairly Hard	20–24 words
Hard	25–28 words
Very Hard	29 words or more

This doesn't mean that every sentence you write should be 15 to 19 words long. That would be boring. Mix it up, have a few eight word sentences, some 25 word sentences, some 15–19 word sentences, and a few in between. Overall, however, make sure your sentences average in the "fairly easy" to "average" range.

Now try to gauge for yourself how easy a sentence is to read without paying too much attention to its actual length. Place a piece of paper over the right-hand side and rate each sentence as to whether it's average, very easy, easy, fairly easy, fairly hard, hard, or very hard:

Sentences	Degree of Difficulty
I think I'm going to cry.	easy
Although you haven't been with us very long, you can probably see by everything that goes on here that we are in deep trouble.	fairly difficult
It really looks like Johnny will be in trouble before he finishes this performance.	fairly easy
When a car hits yours head-on it drives you upon your steering wheel and column.	average
So the beginner who is not a beginner but something of a hot-shot back home on the packed down trails he is used to adjusts his goggles and his white-silk scarf, brings his right thumb and forefinger together gallantly and steels his nerve.	hard

Sentences	Degree of Difficulty
Rapid growth calls for rapid building.	easy
The "ghost town" is a distinctive American institution in which whole communities have packed up and moved on, thriving only in distant memory.	fairly hard
Robert had often experienced the tragedy of others.	easy
The older infant wants to manipulate objects such as cradle gyms he can pull on and swat at.	average
Last June, in the famous New York City's Bronx, the doors opened on the Lilia Acheson Wallace World of Birds.	average (count the name as one word unless extremely long)

COME TO THE POINT IMMEDIATELY

Can you imagine plowing through sentence after sentence without finding out what the point is? I won't do it and you probably won't, either. Yet, writers frequently run five, six, seven and more paragraphs before they let their reader know what they're talking about. This is foolish. After all, it's extremely difficult to hold a person's attention anytime. In writing, it's doubly difficult because all that reader has to do is shift his eyes and he's gone.

For instance, Roger Billings, who owned a part-time mail order business, wrote two different direct mail pieces for a novelty pencil sharpener, each of which he mailed to 500 potential customers. In the first he talked about the benefits of a good pencil sharpener in a rambling way and didn't mention the sharpener itself until the fifth sentence. The second started out by simply saying: You can now buy an unusual novelty pencil sharpener. Then he went on to explain the other details. The second ad pulled three times as many responses as the first and made Roger well over $1800.

Because readers pay more attention when you come to the point immediately, it is vital to quickly tell your reader what you intend to say. If possible, do it in the first sentence. If that isn't practical, then try to state your point within the first paragraph. The rule is this: Decide what the reader wants to know and state that first, then fill in the remaining details in logical order.

Now, let's see if you can handle a few of these rambling beginnings. Look through the sentences on the left, (put a piece of paper over the answers on the right) and see if you can make those sentences readable.

The Rambling Way

The papers that won the poetry contest were marked with a big red X and put on the board at the front of the room; the rest were stacked in a neat pile at the back. There was a lot of talk about canceling, but several of the teachers talked to the principal and he finally decided not to. The poetry contest itself was held Saturday and about 200 people came. I think Bill James, Tom Jordan, and Mary Halverston finally won.

It is difficult to put the Easy Master table together unless you have the proper light. The box looks like it doesn't contain enough parts but it does. If you will follow instructions on page four it will go together easily.

An eminent person asked to itemize the qualities demanded by his own work or by any task which he supervises names every desirable trait, partly because every job he does requires all, but in different degrees. The only sound procedure, that of measuring persons of proved accomplishment and so determining empirically what differentiates them from others is not always possible.

The "Right" Way

(Decide what the reader wants to know, state that, then fill in the details in some order.) *Bill James, Tom Jordan and Mary Halverston won last Saturday's poetry contest.* The winning poems were displayed on the board at the front of the room, the rest were stacked in a neat pile at the back. At one time it was thought the contest might be canceled, but since 200 people came, the teachers talked to the principal, and it was allowed to continue.

To put your Easy Master table together, simply follow the instructions on page four. The Easy Master package contains all the parts you will need. For easy assembly, put it together in the proper light.

Only one or two traits are really necessary in handling any particular job or task. Most eminent people, however, list many desirable traits when asked to decide what qualities are demanded by their own work. Actually, the only sound way to do this—although not always possible—is to measure persons of proved accomplishment and determine how they differ from other people.

JUST TELL YOUR READER ABOUT IT

This is an extremely important rule. If you want to write plainly you can do so by talking to your reader as if he were sitting across from you. How you do it will probably depend on whom you're talking to, but it should be plain and easy to understand. That doesn't mean you must omit key elements. By all means, keep all necessary words, but if the final version doesn't sound like the way you'd talk to another person, then say it another way. After that, if you're still not satisfied it's really conversational and easy to understand, illustrate the point with some examples.

Now let's see if we can put a few of these principles into actual practice. Here's one: *The effective execution of every business and industrial task requires training during which a novice accepts in pay more than he produces.*

This isn't good communication. And if you expect most people to understand you, you've got to make it conversational like this: *It is necessary to have some training for almost every job and during the training period probably no beginning worker is really worth what he gets.*

What we really did was to connect up the basic ideas in a simpler, more understandable way. In addition we put some of these concepts into different terms. The basic idea is to express it, more or less the way you'd say it face to face with someone else.

If you have trouble doing this, go off by yourself, imagine somebody is sitting across from you, and say it out loud, then go back and write it that way.

Let's try one more: *Those with the measurable traits of potential salesmen should be recognized and given opportunity where feasible to encounter the buying world.*

All right, in conversation you probably wouldn't say, "the measurable traits of a potential salesmen." You'd probably say, "with the potential to be a salesman." And you probably wouldn't say, "where feasible to encounter the buying world."

You should simply say: *Anyone with the potential to be a salesman should be recognized and given a chance to sell.* This sentence holds your reader and makes him easily understand because the flavor is familiar. This familiar, conversational tone always has impact. Now try a bit of this.

Try making the sentences on the left as conversational as possible. When finished check them with ours.

Stiff Writing	**Conversational Writing**
Escape as we use it here means a shift of pace and attitude from the nearly all-embracing domain of work.	Escape means not taking work so seriously, and also slowing down, and not working quite as hard.
Some people find in "dime" novels, cockfighting, trotting races, in barbershop song, a variant from the working role.	Some people escape from the boredom of their work with the "dime" novel, cockfighting, trotting races, and barbershop singing.
Likewise much time in the office itself is spent in sociability, making good will tours, talking to salesmen, joshing secretaries.	In the office you frequently chat with the people nearby, visit with others around the office, flirt with the secretaries, or talk to the salesmen who come in.
The seasonal and geographic limitations that in the earlier period narrowed food variations for all but the very rich have now been largely done away with by the network of distribution and the techniques of food preservation.	Because we can now keep food longer and get it there faster people can have almost any kind of fresh food they want no matter what time of year it is or where they live.
There are many managers who do not content themselves with allowing top management and the personnel department to tell workers that they have a stake in the output and that their work is important.	Although a lot of companies try, as official policy, to get across the idea that work is important and really means something to the worker, many managers feel this isn't enough and believe they too should personally try to put this idea across to the people who work for them.

KEEP THE ESSENTIALS AND MAKE IT SIMPLE IN BETWEEN

Even though some writing is complicated and technical, it needn't be hard to understand. It simply requires the application of the plain talk principles.

Instead of using a simple explanation, however, most of us work hard to make our sentences indirect and complicated. We must stop this. The rule is: Say it in a conversational way between the needed technical terms. Let's take an example:

If there is more than one catch basin being used per operation, the catch basins should be monitored relative to the amount of foreign material in them, and a large screen should be placed over each opening in relationship to the size of the materials within each basin. If materials continue to contaminate the downflow afterwards, it is due to deterioration of screening quality.

This isn't very readable, and it doesn't use plain talk. Yet, certainly not because it couldn't.

The problem is that the writer got carried away and failed to say the things in between the needed technical items clearly. This is pretty easy to clear up, however. Simply decide what you need to tell your reader and say the rest of it as though you were talking to him in conversation.

If you have more than one catch basin and foreign material keeps getting in, then you should place a screen over each opening. The screen, of course, should keep out any of the material that might fall in the basin. If material still falls in the basin after you've installed the screens, then you'd better look closely to make sure the screens themselves are in good shape.

The words *monitored, relative, relationship* are absolutely unnecessary and are just thrown in by the writer because he thinks he needs this tone. He doesn't, and simply makes his writing hard to understand.

George Randolph, a Cincinnati factory worker recently promoted to supervisor, decided that since he was now part of the management team he should also upgrade all his reports and memos. As a result, instead of simply saying exactly what he meant, George made even the simplest instructions difficult, make them as fancy and complicated as possible. The first week on the job he issued written job instructions to one of the crews and went on to another piece of work. Checking a week later he discovered, much to his horror, that the crew couldn't understand what he had said, tried to complete the work anyway, and had made several serious mistakes, costing in the neighborhood of $65,000.

Being an intelligent man, George realized immediately what had happened and decided to correct the mistake. From then on his memos and orders were as clear as he could make them. At the end of the year the company awarded George a $2000 bonus because his clear, concise memos and other written material had resulted in many thousands of dollars of savings to that company.

Now let's see if we can take some of this unnecessary technical material and uncomplicate it:

Technical	Uncomplicated
Learning is a process of gaining or changing insights, or thought patterns.	Learning is the process of gaining a new way of looking at something or of understanding it. It can also be changing the way you think about things.
If children are basically active their underlying characteristics are inborn, thus psychological reality comes from within them.	If children are active they are born with certain traits. And the way they look at things actually comes from within them.
A theory of learning not only reflects an assumption concerning the basic nature of man, it also represents a psychological system or outlook. Or to say this another way, each systematic psychological system or basic outlook has its unique approach to learning.	The theory of learning assumes basic things about man and also represents a particular way of looking at something.

GRAMMAR DOESN'T COUNT

The name of the game in word power dynamics is *communication*. In order to produce the greatest impact you must get across your ideas as rapidly and with as much understanding as possible. This means it's okay to use any natural straightforward method that gets the job done.

As a result there are some favorite rules of grammarians that you must now learn to ignore. The first of these is *never end a sentence with a preposition*. Actually, prepositions at the end of a sentence make it simpler and more familiar sounding to the reader. For this reason they should be used. There's nothing at all wrong with a sentence which says: *This is an assumption not everybody may be ready to go along with. This is the thing we came here for. It was a greater triumph than he had ever hoped for,* etc. Also, if you listen to grammarians they tell you never to use the split infinitive, yet this form works well in communication. A split infinitive, of course, is created by simply placing some kind of a modifying word between the preposition and the verb form. Like this: He is now ready *(to* quickly *gather)* all the crops from the field. Grammarians tell us it should be *to gather quickly,* but in many cases that makes the phrase awkward.

There are other rules, but it's not necessary to list them, for today there is a considerable difference between theoretical grammar and practical English. Simple, plain English communicates well; theoretical English gets in the way. So forget about parts of speech and rules of grammar and simply communicate in a natural easy way.

Now here are some general rules for anyone who wants to write in plain language and likes to be direct, simple, brief, vigorous, and lucid. They have been around a long time and are as follows:

1. Prefer the familiar word to the farfetched.
2. Prefer the concrete word to the abstract.
3. Prefer the single word to a group of words meaning the same thing.
4. Prefer the short word to the long.
5. Prefer the Saxon word to the Romance word.

I have a few arguments with this, but in general they are good principles to follow.

TAKE OUT ALL UNNECESSARY WORDS

Plain talk demands effective communication. Unfortunately, anytime you use more words than necessary to put the point across you are making that writing harder to read, and if you put in enough unnecessary words, you can, as before, completely stop your reader. The trick is to push your thoughts together—weed out all extra words—and keep only those needed to communicate clearly and effectively.

The authority on this is Rudolf Flesch, and if you would like a more detailed explanation of how to save words than is offered here consult his excellent book, A *New Guide to Better Writing*, Rudolf Flesch and A.H. Lass, Popular Library.

Here, however, are the basics:

1. *Say the same thing only once:* Amazingly enough, we often use two words in the same sentence that have the same meaning. For instance, someone writes: *I'd like to have you come and visit me this weekend.* Yet, the words *to come* and the word *visit* mean almost the same thing, so the sentence should be written: *I'd like to have you visit me this weekend.* This hasn't changed the meaning one bit, yet it's taken out two words the reader doesn't have to read through. There are many of these. You won't ever get them all. But try when possible to use just the necessary words.

2. *Cut down clauses.* Clauses are often like single words. Many people put in many more than necessary out of habit. Yet you can nearly always put your point across more effectively if you eliminate those that don't contribute to the meaning. For instance, someone writes: *Our friend, who was a big bragger, lived next door.* The clause, who was a big bragger, can certainly be cut down without changing the meaning. It should read: *Our friend, a big bragger, lived next door.*

   Here's another: *Any person who has a college education can do that job.* This is a little more complicated, but the *who has* can be eliminated easily, so take it out, combine the rest, and write: *Any college-educated person can do that job.* It's also possible to turn a subordinate clause into a prepositional phrase, making it both more readable and saving words. For instance: *When you come to the library, turn left and drive three blocks.* You can put the same meaning across by saying, *At the library turn left and drive three blocks.* Here's another: *As soon as John comes home we will leave.* You can save words by saying: *When John comes home we will leave.*

Now let's try it. Eliminate the unnecessary clauses and cut the writing to its briefest form. Put a piece of paper over the right-hand answers before you try.

With Unnecessary Clause	Cut Down
Our friend, *who was the high school principal*, came to our house last night.	Our friend, the high school principal, came to our house last night.
Jim Jones, the man *who owns the local grocery store*, went on a trip to Spain.	Jim Jones, the local grocery store owner, took a trip to Spain.
My girl friend, *who has been away at college*, dropped into my apartment last night.	My girl friend, back from college, dropped into my apartment last night.
Billie, *who left early*, never did come home.	Billie left early and never did come home.
Any person *who is a friend of John's* is a friend of mine.	Any friend of John's is a friend of mine.
We'll be ready as soon as you finish that project.	We'll be ready when you finish that project.
We'll be ready to go by the time you finish that project.	We'll be ready to go when you finish that project.
In order to get the most out of this lesson you must study it thoroughly.	To get the most out of this lesson you must study it thoroughly.
He went to school so that he could become a doctor.	He went to school to become a doctor.

3. *Say It Directly:* Much writing is confusing because the thought does not go directly in a straight line from one end of a sentence to another. Anytime you take your reader on a roundabout path, you slow the writing down and make it boring and difficult. Therefore ask yourself, "Is this the most direct way to say what I've written, and is the main thought a straight line from one end of the sentence to the other?" Some sentences, of course, won't lend themselves to this treatment, but others will. To do this, often you will need to change the ending of at least one word in that sentence.

　　　Now, if someone writes: *They gave us a welcome that warmed our hearts*, they are taking the reader on a circular path. To fix the sentence, change the ending of the word "warm," combine it with hearts, and zero right into the point like this: *They gave us a heartwarming welcome.* One more: *They welcomed the boss at the station with an enthusiasm that amazed everybody.* The first part is very direct. The second part isn't. Change the word *amazed* to *amazing* and write the sentence in a straight line: *They welcomed the boss at the station with amazing enthusiasm.* Now try it yourself.

Slow Sentence	Direct Sentence
Not everybody likes it when he has to shop in a store that is crowded.	Not everybody likes to shop in a crowded store.
I was waiting at the counter for my wife until I became impatient.	Waiting at the counter for my wife, I grew impatient.
That was a dinner I could really enjoy.	That was a really enjoyable dinner.
That was a girl who was a delight.	That was a delightful girl.
He was held prisoner in a room without windows.	He was held prisoner in a windowless room.
We woke up to a sky without any clouds.	We woke up to a cloudless sky.
The road was not crowded at all.	That road was uncrowded.
I could tell that he was far from being happy.	I could tell that he was unhappy.
He stared at me with an expression that showed astonishment.	He stared at me in astonishment.
He bought a boat that had been built by hand.	He bought a handbuilt boat.

In short then, the real *word power secret* is to write plainly and simply, keep sentence length in check, come to the point immediately, be conversational, and write in a direct, straightforward manner. Anything else causes the reader to work harder than is really necessary. And if we are going to eventually utilize all the word power principles we must first make sure we are communicating effectively with our readers.

IN CONCLUSION

This is the age of written communication. Unfortunately much of it is bad. Many problems can be eliminated, however, if you simply learn to utilize plain talk. Do this by (1) checking your writing with a readability index, making sure you stay within the "average" range, (2) keeping your sentence length in check, (3) coming to the point immediately, and (4) weeding out all unnecessary words.

1. *Use a Readability Index.* A readability guide that works well is to count the number of sentences in a sample of 100 words. Divide the number of sentences into 100, count all the words over seven letters in length, then add both figures together and divide by two. The piece of writing that rates between 12 and 16 is easily readable.
2. *Keep sentence length in check.* Sentences should average about 15 words. Mix them up, however, Have some eight word sentences, some 25 word sentences, some 15–19 word sentences, and a few in between.
3. *Come to the point immediately.* Simply decide what your reader wants to know, state that point, then fill in the details in order.
4. *Just talk to your reader.* Instead of using stilted roundabout talk in your writing, simply write as if you were talking to someone who was sitting across from you.
5. *Keep the essentials.* To make technical material easily understandable keep the important technical terms and put the rest in simple conversational English.
6. *Don't worry about grammar.* Simple, clear communication is more important than grammar. If a sentence or phrase can be understood clearly, by all means use it even if it violates some rules of grammar. Here are the rules of clear communication:
   1. Prefer the familiar word to the farfetched.
   2. Prefer the concrete word to the abstract.
   3. Prefer the single word to a group of words meaning the same thing.
   4. Prefer the short word to the long.
   5. Prefer the Saxon word to the Romance word.

7. *Take out all unnecessary words.* Too many words make it difficult for your reader to grasp the point easily. To cure this:

    a. *Say the same thing only once.* Often we use two words in the same sentence that have a similar meaning. Take out one, and use just those words necessary to make your point.

    b. *Cut down clauses.* Eliminate clauses that don't contribute to the meaning and cut the writing to its briefest form.

    c. *Say it directly.* Much writing takes your reader on a circular path. This can be corrected by changing the word ending, then condensing the sentence.

How to Control and Personally Benefit from Every Moment of Your Time*

14

I well remember the first time I actually kept a diary of where the time went. It surprised me and it surprised my fellow managers. We were responding to a request from our executive that we log up our time for a week and then compare notes. It was suggested that we list our major activities and make a note about every hour in a time diary. Some of the headings I used were: "Answering the Telephone," "Reviewing Routine Reports," "Shooting the Breeze," and "Miscellaneous." I added to the list as time went on because when I checked myself to find out what I was doing, I would sometimes identify a significant new activity.

The first surprise came to me on the matter of the telephone. Because of its ubiquitous way of interrupting my work, I had imagined that the telephone took about 25% of my time. The fact was that it took only 5%.

The second surprise came when we compared notes the following week. I found that I was putting about three times as much time into correspondence than were my fellow managers. That gave me food for thought, and I decided to cool it a bit. Now that I think back, there was probably some private desire to achieve a writing career and I probably liked to see myself in print. Although this is appropriate now for my

---

*Sydney F. Love, *Mastery and Management of Time* (Englewood Cliffs, N.J.: Prentice-Hall, Inc., 1978).

career as a consultant, it was not appropriate when I was a manager of engineering.

A SENSE OF THE VALUE OF TIME

Ron is a business associate of mine in Los Angeles who supplies office services to a number of associations. A few years ago I proposed to him a new kind of seminar which might not make much money in the beginning, but which had a great potential for development. Ron lacked enthusiasm for the project and when I pushed for a decision, this is what he said. "Syd, your idea sounds O.K. to me, but right now I have several other opportunities which have much more profit and excitement in them. Besides, since they're my ideas, I would much prefer to do them anyway. I've only got so much time to spread around on different projects and right now I've got better fish to fry. For example, I am behind on writing up minutes for association meetings for which they pay me $50 an hour. With a little effort I can line up more work like that and it will pay me much more than that seminar. Frankly Syd, I've got more valuable uses for my time right now."

"Well, I can see your point of view, Ron, and if it's not worth your time, it's probably not worth my time either, I'll look for something better to do with my time too."

Ron is a dedicated and hard-working businessman and he thrives on accomplishment. It just so happens that money is one of the measures that he gets on accomplishment. But there's more to it than that. He doesn't take on any money job that comes along; he reserves his precious time for those things that serve his overall purposes best. He operates on the *Time Awareness Principle* which is described in this chapter.

Benefits You Will Obtain from Using the Time Awareness Principle

When you understand and apply the Time Awareness Principle, you will be fully aware that your time is precious—for, like a moonbeam reflected in a cat's eye, it will soon be gone forever. Whenever there is something that you wish to accomplish time has value to you because of an essential tradeoff.

Time is a nonrenewable resource. We all get 24 hours a day of it. Some achieve things with their time and others get nothing for it. If you have no sense of time, then it merely floats by in an endless stream, like water down the Mississippi; you may lead a quiet and peaceful existence, but that is all. The joys of accomplishment and the joys of having a good time can be yours but you must first realize that time can be spent only once. Then you will want to spend it wisely.

Benefits of the Time Awareness Principle:

1. You will develop a sense of the importance of time and become aware of what you are doing with this scarce resource.
2. You will know how to avoid wasting time that can be better used elsewhere because you will understand the fundamental relationship of time to performance and cost.
3. You will know that your time has monetary value, and what price to put on it.

How to Obtain the Benefits

This chapter is an explanation of the Time Awareness Principle. Come back to the principle frequently and apply it to time-saving situations of your own. When you understand the principle thoroughly you too can become the inventor of time-saving techniques.

To help you understand the principle, there is an example from everyday life on how you can apply it to having your car washed, and another on arranging lunch. Then I'll show you six techniques managers and executives can use to employ the Time Awareness Principle. You will be shown how to find out where your time goes. You will see how the principle can be applied to: reading reports, varying the quality of letters, handling unwanted telephone calls, and presenting at a meeting. Finally, I'll tell you what you can do today to use the Purpose Principle for the mastery of time.

Take a little time while reading this chapter to understand thoroughly the *fundamental tradeoff of time with performance and cost. It is the secret of good time management.* The tradeoff arises out of my scientific reasoning about the relationship of time to purpose. It is explained in everyman's language, and once you understand it, you will find the other principles in the book easy to understand and apply.

THE TIME AWARENESS PRINCIPLE

Time Has Value When There Is a Purpose

When there is a purpose, there is a fundamental tradeoff of performance, time and cost. By *performance*, P, I mean the attributes of the new state of affairs brought about by an activity or task being done to serve some purpose. If your purpose is accomplished by the production of a new machine, then we may talk about its performance attributes or its results. If, on the other hand, the purpose is accomplished by participation in some experience, then performance will refer to the quality of the experience. In other words, if we are to accomplish our purpose, then some object or experience is produced. That object or experience has attributes which we can call the performance, although in some cases we may mean the performance level, or the results, or the accomplishment or the experience.

The *cost*, C, will mean any money which is employed to bring about the new state of affairs, such as money for materials, money to buy other persons' time, money for travel, and in some cases even the value of talent which could be used elsewhere. Our cost term might be looked upon as the sum total of the resources which are required to "put the show on the road," so to speak.

The *time*, T, is the number of hours or days or months actually devoted to the accomplishment of a specific activity or task. It is your personal possession of time that you may use effectively or wastefully.

If you work on tasks towards some purpose, then there will be some level of performance achieved, some cost or use of resources, and definitely some use of time. We are now ready for a concise statement of the principle.

The Time Awareness Principle

Given that the level of performance, P, and the amount of cost, C, remain within satisfactory limits, then time, T, can be traded off for either of these. If more time is put in, the cost may be less or performance may be higher. Less time can be used if you accept a lower level of performance or are prepared for higher cost.

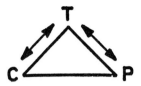

Love's Tradeoff Rule:

Trade time for performance or cost on one task, and obtain more for that time by applying it to something of more utility. The performance and cost should remain within satisfactory limits.

Since time can be traded for the cost or resources and used in accomplishing something, then *time has actual monetary value.* The value of time to you will depend on how you can save money by using your time on various tasks which contribute to your purposes. The example below will clarify the meaning of this principle.

Using the Time Awareness Principle in Everyday Life

Getting my car washed: a tradeoff of time for quality or money. Every once in a while I get the notion that my purposes would be better served by showing up at a client's place with a good clean car. In time-management terms, what I want to accomplish is the possession of a clean car. In plain words, the car needs a wash. This happened to me on a pleasant Saturday afternoon in May after several days of rain and muddy streets. I thought to myself, "I can wash my car myself, presumably at a very low cost, since I do have the resources of a hose and a brush. However, I'll need to use some of my time and there are better things that I could be doing. On the other hand, I might be able to cajole one of my sons into washing the car. But if I do I will have to fork out a substantial cash donation. Moreover, I probably won't be satisfied with the quality of the result because he will be in a hurry. Things were better when he had to borrow the car from me but now he has his own. Now it's an uphill battle to get mine cleaned because he's so busy polishing his own.

"Alternatively, I could drive my car down to a car wash and pay a dollar extra on my gas and have it washed in one of those 'quickies.' Still, it may not be so quick because it's a Saturday afternoon and there will be a big lineup of cars. Besides that, I would have to drive it there and back. Not only that but the car wash I would get from one of those roller brush machines is not of the best quality. The brushes disarrange my windshield washers, they bend my antenna, and the water leaks into my trunk."

I won't tell you what I actually did because that depended on other circumstances which don't enter into your situation. What you see here is that there are many ways to approach a car wash. However, given some kind of external circumstances, one of the three things— performance, P, time, T, or cost, C, will dominate. I might have been in a hurry and time dominated. Or I might have been short of pocket money and traded my time for money saved. If it was a weekday and the gas station was not busy, I may have traded off some money to save myself some time. In each case something would have dominated the situation and enabled me to decide what to do and what kind of tradeoff to take. Mind you, if I didn't have something better to do with my time, then time itself would not have been a factor. That is not the way it was. Time is always important to me because it's only here once.

Sometimes time dominates the tradeoff. Let's take a look at another example of a situation in which you might get involved. Suppose you think about ways to accomplish the task of having your noon meal during a work day. You could go to a nice restaurant. In that case the performance or quality of the experience will dominate over the time and cost. We can write this P/TC. On the other hand, you might drive home for 25 cents and have a meal there, in which the cost dominates. You could write this as C/T with P not being important either way. Another possibility would be to bring your own lunch and eat it in your office. In this case it could be that both time and cost dominate the performance or quality of the experience. We can write this TC/P.

In a case where time alone dominated, you might order a snack sent up to your office—anything that's available. Then we could write T/CP. We have covered four ways for you to have a noonday meal and each requires a different amount of time. What you choose to do will depend on the context and in all cases there will be some tradeoff of time with cost and performance.

Your time has a minimum monetary value. Consider the fact that when there is purpose, your time has some monetary value. For example, if it takes you 15 minutes to wash the car and you save $1, then maybe it's worth $4 an hour. In the noon meal case, if you get the same refreshing experience by having a meal at home as you do at a restaurant, and you can save $2 by taking an extra 20 minutes for a home lunch, then the time value would work out at $6 an hour. The value of your time depends on what you can trade it for in terms of resources; that is, what you can gain or keep from spending. In business they put it this way: The cost of doing one thing is equal to the profit that could have been gained from doing another. It is the "lost opportunity cost."

What is your time worth to your employer? If your salaried time is $15 an hour, it is actually costing your employer about $30 an hour, if the overhead is included. If you have opportunities to do moonlighting in your spare time, then you are not working on a fixed income and your other time has a minimum value—let's say, for example, $5 an hour. This is the value you would apply to your discretionary time, as you cannot charge yourself for time to eat meals, time to sleep, and time to make love. So the average person has at least 3 hours a day of discretionary time which should be given a monetary value if it could otherwise be put to earning or saving some money.

As for myself, I have put a flat rate of $20 an hour on my uncommitted time because that is its minimum economic value to me if I use it for teaching or writing. This means that I am prepared to spend money to be where the action is, and not waste time doing ordinary things or watching ordinary shows and movies. I will spend money to charter a yacht for a few days rather than spend weeks of leisure with nothing exciting to do. I try to do as many worthwhile and interesting things as I can in the time available to me, whether it be productive work, recreation or mind relaxation.

4 WAYS TO MAKE THIS PRINCIPLE WORK FOR YOU

1. Reading Routine Reports: Some Activities Deserve More Time Than Others

Take a look at some routine work you do, like checking daily time cards or daily progress reports. Are you getting good value for the time you devote to it? If you reduce the amount of time involved and just scan for major errors, will this be sufficient? If it is, then you can trade time for a small loss in performance and put that time to something of greater value. In other words, to save time on some routine task you ask yourself if you can reduce the time at some small loss of performance and then invest the time better elsewhere instead of spending it on additional work of low value.

Here is how I reasoned it out with a sales manager at a workshop in Toronto: A routine sales report can seldom be done to perfection. No matter how often you check and review it, there will still be errors or improvements that can be made. In other words, the performance level of the completed task (the quality, reliability, etc.) is variable. Thus, if you accept that the performance is less than 100%, you can then accept 95% performance level and save about 50% of the time. The saved time can have more value if put into another activity—like selling!

2. Relative Quality of Letters: Put Your Heroic Effort Where It Counts

Let's examine an intermittent bit of work, such as writing non-routine letters. If you write a letter to a supplier to get some information on a new product, you can probably do a fast job because the supplier is going to fill your request whether your letter is great or not. You can trade time for performance.

If you have been asked to compose a letter for your president about a problem that you have been investigating, you will probably put quite a bit of time into it, and performance will dominate over time. **You are aware, though, that your time is important and you're going to put it on the important letters and cut it down on the less important ones.** Don't waste it on trivia! The benefit will be from switching your effort to the important things.

As a matter of fact, you could go one step further on the purchasing letter. You could circle a reader inquiry number on a card in a trade journal instead of sending a letter. If you have a secretary, you could just mark the magazine "write for info on this" and let her send a form letter. Looking again at the letter to the president, you may be short of the time you need to do an adequate job. Therefore you invest more resources in it, have a subordinate draft up what is required and you simply polish off the final copy.

Now you are being aware of time. You can gain time by using resources. You can gain time by dropping performance. Or both. Of course, if you have nothing else to do, then the time saved isn't worth a wooden nickel, but most managers and executives that I know are harried all the time. The nature of their work is so varied, however, that they are able to trade off time on one task to use on another, e.g., less time on a meeting and more on a new proposal.

3. Telephone Interruptions:
Limiting the Effect on Your Time

Sure, the telephone interrupts you. You cannot be sure whether it is important or not. You can't live in suspense, so you answer it—thereby falling into the telephone company's sucker trap. They make you think it is a sin not to answer the telephone.

Many persons have solved this problem by having their calls screened. A call can be more important than what you are doing, but every once in a while a colleague gets through with a bag of wind. How do you get control of this time for your important work? Easy. Be frank and firm—unless you are prepared to give away the time forever in exchange for some hot air.

Six Ways to Limit the Effect of Unwanted
Telephone Interruptions

1. Tell a long-winded caller that you are busy on some pressing work and that you will be able to call back later. Then call when he is about to leave his office for the day. The conversation will be short.

2. Ask your caller for an estimate of the time required. Then negotiate!

3. Steer your caller on to the problem you are working on. "By the way, George, have you any good ideas on how to . . ." You might get help, but the real name of the game is to get your caller hung up on something he really can't answer.

4. You give your secretary a signal to leave her desk and call you from another place. "Hold on there, George, I have a call on the other line and my secretary is away. Can I take it?"

5. If the call is through a switchboard, you can signal your secretary to arrange for a disconnect in the middle of your sentence. You can do this with an outside caller who can't clobber you—like the salesman who bluffed his way past your secretary's screening. You can do this in an emergency—once. After that your conscience will force you to use your talking skill instead.

6. You can read while you listen—a coward's way of minimizing the bruises to your time management by a wind-bag who should have his calls taped and played back to him!

4. Preparation of a Presentation: Using the Time Awareness Principle on Meetings

Let's look at a group activity. You have been asked to give a briefing at a meeting about your new project. **The higher the quality of the briefing, the more time or resources you must employ.** If your boss and your boss's boss are going to be there at the briefing, then you will probably feel that performance dominates over time, provided that the time for preparation remains reasonable. Cost also dominates time because we will imagine that your expense budget is really tight. You don't think that you can afford a full color video-tape production of your project to be made and presented at the briefing. Tough! No matter how good you want to be on the performance or time, there's always a tradeoff to be made. Right? In this case, you had better put extra time into making a good impression and take the time away from something that doesn't require top-notch performance.

ANALYZING YOUR TIME EXPENDITURE

Many, many persons have reported that **they were surprised to find out where the time was actually going as compared with their perception of it.** Nothing speaks more loudly or eloquently than hard facts. Try it.

You must make a determined effort to analyze where the time went as soon after something happens as you can. Take a sheet of paper and list upon it the kinds of things you do. After that, list some of the time-consuming ways of doing them. For example, you can list things such as communicating upwards, putting out brush fires, long-range planning, and chit-chat. You can also list ways of spending time on them, such as telephone time, correspondence time, writing reports, attending meetings, and so forth. After a few tries, you will develop a good framework for recording the actual use of your time, such as that shown in Figure 1. For each day, record in quarter hours where the significant time went. Record your time usage for at least a week. Add up the times in these activities and compare what you were *actually* doing with what you *should* have been doing.

What may surprise you is the amount of time that goes into what we call chit-chat, chewing the fat, or shooting the breeze. Chatting is inevitable and probably good for your occupation, but you can decide how much of your time should go into it. If you want to manage time, you must first find out where the time is going. Only then will you be able to take effective action.

How to Accomplish More Through Time Awareness

Some of your time goes into work activities, a significant proportion goes into personal maintenance activities, and a portion goes into relaxation and pleasure. Something which is easily confirmed by observation is that most managers and executives overlap their work time and personal time. For example, an executive may leave the office early for a game of golf and then spend two hours in the evening on some business correspondence. It appears to some that they are "workaholics"; that is, they work all the time. By and large most of them lead a balanced life, with accomplishment being the main goal. You will accomplish more if you use all of your 24 hours effectively.

You can take the Time Awareness Principle and extend it to activities and tasks on the personal side. You can take your routine tasks and classify them for the dominance of either performance, cost, or time. You can also take each intermittent task as it comes along and consider whether or not there is a dominance of one of these factors.

As you practice looking at your activities and tasks, you will become intensely aware of the value of time. You will think in advance along these lines: "How much of my time is it worth to put into this, giving consideration to the other valuable tradeoffs I can make with my time?"

ACTIVITY / WAY	COMMUNICATING UPWARDS			LONG RANGE PLANNING		PUTTING OUT BRUSH FIRES		CHIT – CHAT					
	M	T	W										
MEETINGS	1	0	0	0	1/2	3	1	1/2	0	1/4			
	T 1/2	F S 1/4		2	1/4	2	3 3/4	3/4	1	0			
CORRESPONDENCE	day of week					time spent to nearest 1/4 hour							
TELEPHONE CALLS													
TOTALS													

Figure 1: Find Out Where Your Time Is Going

GUIDE TO TIME MASTERY

The Time Awareness Principle:

Given that the level of performance (P), and the amount of cost (C), are both within reasonable limits, then time (T), can be traded off for either of these. If more time is put into it then the cost may be less or the performance may be higher. Less time can be used if you accept a lower level of performance or are more prepared to put in more resources (cost).

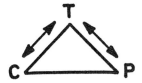

Main Points

1. Time is valuable because it is a tradeoff with cost.
2. Time gained by a tradeoff with performance or cost in one task may be better used on another task. (Otherwise part of it is "wasted.")
3. Routine tasks generally fall into patterns where either P, C, or T dominates.
4. Intermittent tasks will have a dominance of P, C, or T, depending on the situation.

WHAT YOU SHOULD DO TODAY TO START ACCOMPLISHING MORE WITH YOUR TIME

1. Identify three important tasks which were completed in the past week. For each of these, in the light of experience, which should have dominated—performance, cost, or time?
2. List three tasks which are ahead of you. Consider the situation and specify which will dominate—performance, cost, or time?

3. Can you save time in one of the above tasks by trading it with performance or cost and put the time to better use on one of the other tasks?

4. Calculate the average daily time spent on the maintenance task of eating. Now estimate the amount of time you spend keeping clean and sprucing up. Has performance, cost, or time been dominant in these activities? Do you wish to exchange time between eating and keeping clean? Do you wish to save time on either and put it to use on work-related tasks?

5. Review the specific time mastery techniques in this chapter. Can they be modified for use in your particular work?

TIME CHECKLIST FOR MANAGERS AND EXECUTIVES

Make a checklist of your own activities and tasks on separate sheets of paper. The checklist below will help as a guide. Leave yourself room for additions later.

Activity or Task Descriptions (user to elaborate and enlarge the checklist)

Routine Tasks

MAIL:

- incoming first class
- incoming third class
- incoming subscribed journals for professional development
- incoming trade and business periodicals
- internal letters
- internal reports of peer operations
- daily, weekly, or monthly reports from subordinates
- periodic reports prepared for superiors
- periodic reports for peer operations

CORRESPONDENCE:

- replying to letters
- filing directions for letters
- proofreading typed letters

EXPENSES:

- preparing own expense account
- reviewing expense accounts of others
- administering petty cash fund

OTHER:

- regular local trips
- regular out-of-town trips
- regular telephone reporting

Intermittent Tasks

TELEPHONE:

- taking calls from superiors
- taking calls from peers
- taking calls from subordinates
- taking calls from outsiders
- returning telephone calls

HUMAN RESOURCES:

- recruiting interviews
- work performance reviews
- attending self-development seminars and courses
- resolving personality conflicts
- reprimands
- training of subordinates

OTHER:

- preparation for union negotiations
- special out-of-town trips
- replying to new and unusual letters
- special tasks for superiors
- listening to grapevine information
- unwanted chit-chat
- professional organization work
- reading grievance proceedings

Group Tasks

MEETINGS:

- regular meeting A
- regular meeting B
- regular meeting C
- high priority problem solving meetings
- monthly progress meeting which you call
- informal luncheon meetings
- association meetings
- appointment meetings

OTHER:

- group appraisal of potential recruits
- rehearsals of special presentations
- social activities of work group

Personal Tasks

- eating lunch on work days
- eating home meals
- preparation of home meals
- exercising
- getting ready for bed
- sleeping
- mental relaxation
- physical relaxation
- cleanliness of person
- buying, selecting, and changing clothing
- going to and from work
- professional organization activities
- self development
- reading of nonwork nature
- watching TV
- going to the movies
- maintaining house and car
- gift buying and sending (esp. Christmas)
- socializing with work acquaintances
- socializing with family and personal friends

- major cleanups
- redecorating home
- correspondence
- watching sports
- participating in sports
- telephoning friends
- getting ready to go to work
- pet care (walking dog)
- transporting family members

Do This With Your Checklist

1. For each activity or task on your own prepared checklist, ask yourself, "Can I save time on this by trading time for performance or cost, and put it to better use elsewhere?" Mark as more time or less.

2. Identify those from which time can be borrowed and switched to those that would make better use of your time, in your opinion. Mark them for follow-up action.

Index

N

Needs, physical and ego, 73
New Patterns in Management, 68
Nonverbal observation, 65

O

Objectives:
  keep focused on, 114
  personal, 99
Observation, nonverbal, 65

P

Part of task, 59–60
Patience, aggressive, 169
People:
  adding value, 109
  describing, 104
People-dealing, 176–177
People who can help:
  associate with, 29
  become king, 20
  benefits, 18–20
  boss in house, 20–23
  bridegrooms, 23
  business, 25–26
  control many people, 18
  creative thinker, 24
  energy saved, 19
  find, 18, 20–28
  halfway to success, 19–20
  independent, 24
  industry, 25–27
  insurance salesman, 21
  key man in group, 23–24
  make person the boss, 21
  preacher, salary, 27–28
  promotions refused, 25
  real estate salesman, 22
  relied upon by others, 24
  solve problems, 24
  students, 29
  supervisor caught in middle, 26
  teachers, 28–29
  time saved, 18–19
  use to advantage, 24–25

Personality needs, 178
Personal objectives, 99
Personnel problem, 134–136
Persuasion, 176
Petty thinker, 116
Physical needs, 73
Planning, how much, 109
Plans, outline, 104
Popularity, 38–41
Praise:
  basic desires satisfied, 128
  correct mistakes, 131–133
  encourages others, 104
  every single improvement, 128–129
  feeds ego, 127
  I Am Proud Of You, 123–124
  improvement shown, 125
  instead of criticism, 123
  instead of flattery, 129–131
  makes him feel important, 127
  not just once, 122
  public or private, 125
  releases energy, 127–128
  sincere, 129–131
  study, 124–126
  "Thank you," 129
Preacher, salary, 27–28
Preoccupations, 154
Presentation, timing, 69–70
Problem-solver, 24
Problems, shelving, 56
Procrastination, 59
Product, potential, 143
Progress:
  big thinker, 115
  think, 86–91 (*see also* Leadership)
Promotion, refusal, 25
Proposal, small seeming, 167
Psychological impact, 63

Q

Quarrels, 112
Question-reponse, 65
Questions:
  ask yourself, 34
  convergent, 67, 68
  divergent, 68
  evaluative, 68